ELEMENTS OF LITERATURE

Elements of Literature

JAMES L. POTTER   TRINITY COLLEGE

THE ODYSSEY PRESS · INC · NEW YORK

ACKNOWLEDGMENTS

The author wishes to thank the following publishers for permission to reprint excerpts from copyrighted works in this volume:

Harcourt, Brace & World, Inc. Excerpts from the poem "Junk" by Richard Wilbur, from the *Collected Poems of Richard Wilbur.*

Holt, Rinehart and Winston, Inc. Excerpts from the following poems by Robert Frost: "Stopping by Woods on a Snowy Evening," "After Apple-Picking," "Come In," and the complete poem "Fire and Ice," all from *Complete Poems of Robert Frost.* Copyright 1923, 1930, 1939 by Holt, Rinehart and Winston, Inc. Copyright 1942, 1951, © 1958 by Robert Frost. Copyright © 1967 by Lesley Frost Ballantine. Reprinted by permission of Holt, Rinehart and Winston, Inc. Excerpts from "With Rue My Heart Is Laden," by A. E. Housman, from "A Shropshire Lad" – Authorized Edition – from *The Collected Poems of A. E. Housman.* Copyright 1939, 1940, © 1959 by Holt, Rinehart and Winston, Inc. Copyright © 1967 by Robert E. Symons. Reprinted by permission of Holt, Rinehart and Winston, Inc.

The Macmillan Company. Excerpts from "The Second Coming" by William Butler Yeats. Printed by permission of The Macmillan Company from *Later Poems* by William Butler Yeats. Copyright The Macmillan Company 1924 and renewed in 1952 by Bertha Georgie Yeats. Excerpts from "Sailing to Byzantium" by William Butler Yeats. Printed by permission of The Macmillan Company from *Collected Poems* by William Butler Yeats. Copyright The Macmillan Company 1928 and renewed in 1956 by Georgie Yeats. Excerpts from "Cargoes" by John Masefield. From *The Story of a Round House* by John Masefield. Copyright 1912 by The Macmillan Company, renewed in 1940 by John Masefield.

The Society of Authors. Excerpts from "With Rue My Heart Is Laden," by A. E. Housman. Permission granted by the Society of Authors as the literary representative of the Estate of the late A. E. Housman, and Messrs. Jonathan Cape, Ltd., publishers of A. E. Housman's *Collected Poems.*

A. P. Watt & Son. Excerpts from "The Second Coming" and "Sailing to Byzantium" by William Butler Yeats. Reprinted by permission of Mr. M. B. Yeats and the Macmillan Co. of Canada Ltd.

FOR *Judy*

BUT ALSO

Daland

AND

Jonathan

AND EVEN

Holly

Danny

Laurie

Tiki

AND

Katisha

Preface

Elements of Literature is intended to present and briefly explore essential ingredients of the literature of our Western culture. The method usually employed here is as follows. First, the particular "elements" (such as plot and tragic irony) are explained in terms general enough to be widely valid yet specific enough to be useful, each concept being illustrated concisely. Then, in the second half of each chapter, the subtleties and refinements of the elements are surveyed.

The nine chapters fall into four sections according to the kinds of elements dealt with. Chapters 1 (Character) and 2 (Narrative) form the first section, dealing with the "objects" of literature—the characters, settings, and events that constitute the referential material of literature. Chapters 3 (Imagery and Figurative Language), 4 (Sound Effects and Rhythm), and 5 (Style) make up the second section, devoted to the verbal medium of literature—the language elements which differentiate it from other arts. The third section, which deals with the "subjects" of literature, comprises Chapters 6 (Tragedy) and 7 (Comedy), embodying main attitudinal poles, and Chapter 8 (Symbolism), embodying literary meaning or significance. Finally, Chapter 9 (Convention), the fourth section, deals with the cultural framework as it affects literature aesthetically.

The rationale of the analytical approach of *Elements of Literature* is familiar. The text is designed to provide a groundwork of knowledge about elements that compose all our literature without dividing it into genres—poetry, prose fiction, and drama. The generality of such a grounding will make clear the basic unity and parity of all literature that the largely conventional generic divisions tend to obscure. The abstract explanations of literary elements are supplemented by examples of their specific manifestations, to show how the general principles or prototypical phenomena are varied in practice, much as chemical compounds and ions are modifications of elements identified abstractly in the periodic table.

Why is this general and analytic approach desirable? Because an educated person should appreciate literature through an intelligent understanding of it as a whole rather than as a fragmented collection of discrete works. To understand the common denominators of all particular works is to achieve a breadth of knowledge that is the goal of educated men. It produces a richer aesthetic and emotional appreciation of literature and provides the soundest foundation for further literary experience.

Behind this rationale lie certain assumptions that affect the way *Elements of Literature* is used. The first assumption is that literature is primarily an art, and only secondarily a means of communication or a reflection of history or of the author's philosophy. At the same time, literature is art in the sense that it is at least one step back from reality—not a report on actual events but an artificial creation. This esthetic assumption must be made if we are to speak seriously of such things as protagonists, central metaphors, or literary conventions like the proscenium stage, for these are features of the artistic texture and structure of literature, and would be irrelevant or insignificant otherwise.

Another assumption is that the basic, though variable, elements of our literature are to be derived inductively from literary practice; they are not a set of procedures we can deduce from some sort of literary first principles. Consequently, the elements are here offered descriptively rather than prescriptively: these we can observe in various forms in our literature, and no particular form is inherently or necessarily preferable to another (thus, a simple rime scheme is just as good as a complex one, and an isolated symbol just as good as a motif).

This text is intended, then, as a guide to general literary elements, for the purpose of developing an understanding and appreciation of literature as a whole for its own sake as an art. In the discussions of the elements there have been inevitable compromises between precision and definiteness on the one hand, and general validity on the other (hence the frequency of the word "usually" in the text). The particular literary works that the reader will consider in connection with this text will no doubt demonstrate that such compromises are both necessary and most accurate. Just as the plots of different stories never constitute exactly the same pattern and yet are fundamentally similar, so other elements of literature are half-definite yet generally valid concepts. For an accurate aesthetic comprehension and appreciation of literature we become conscious of the general concepts—the common denominators—embodied in the variant particular instances. In so doing, we develop the knowledge and the perception that are the soundest bases for the enjoyment of literature.

As an additional aid to the student, an Appendix is provided that suggests various ways of interpreting a literary work and describes what each method entails. This should serve both students who are preparing a reading assignment in literature and those who are planning to write about a literary work.

J. L. P.

Contents

Contents

Character

BASIC TERMS AND CONCEPTS

CHARACTER

Characters are a basic element in much imaginative literature, and therefore they merit the considerable attention paid to them. When critics speak of a character, they mean any person who figures in a literary work, not particularly a peculiar or eccentric one; sometimes a given character does not actually appear but is merely talked about.

Consider Browning's poem "My Last Duchess"; it is a "dramatic monologue," consisting of the words of one man in a specific situation, as if in a play. The speaker is clearly a character in the work, but he has so much to say about his last Duchess that she, too, becomes a character in the poem, although she never appears or speaks. Furthermore, the Duke aims his speech actively at an envoy from the father of his prospective next Duchess and consequently makes that envoy also a character in the work:

MY LAST DUCHESS

Ferrara

That's my last Duchess painted on the wall,
Looking as if she were alive; I call
That piece a wonder, now: Fra Pandolf's hands
Worked busily a day, and there she stands.
Will't please you sit and look at her? I said
"Fra Pandolf" by design, for never read
Strangers like you that pictured countenance,
The depth and passion of its earnest glance,
But to myself they turned (since none puts by
The curtain I have drawn for you, but I)
And seemed as they would ask me, if they durst,
How such a glance came there; so, not the first
Are you to turn and ask thus. Sir, 'twas not
Her husband's presence only, called that spot
Of joy into the Duchess' cheek: perhaps
Fra Pandolf chanced to say "Her mantle laps
Over my Lady's wrist too much," or "Paint
Must never hope to reproduce the faint
Half-flush that dies along her throat": such stuff
Was courtesy, she thought, and cause enough
For calling up that spot of joy. She had
A heart . . . how shall I say? . . . too soon made glad,
Too easily impressed; she liked whate'er
She looked on, and her looks went everywhere.
Sir, 'twas all one! My favor at her breast,
The dropping of the daylight in the West,
The bough of cherries some officious fool
Broke in the orchard for her, the white mule
·She rode with round the terrace—all and each
Would draw from her alike the approving speech,
Or blush, at least, She thanked men,—good; but thanked
Somehow . . . I know not how . . . as if she ranked
My gift of a nine-hundred-years-old name
With anybody's gift. Who'd stoop to blame
This sort of trifling? Even had you skill
In speech—(which I have not)—to make your will

Quite clear to such an one, and say "Just this
Or that in you disgusts me; here you miss
Or there exceed the mark"—and if she let
Herself be lessoned so, nor plainly set
Her wits to yours, forsooth, and made excuse,
—E'en then would be some stooping, and I choose
Never to stoop. Oh, Sir, she smiled, no doubt,
Whene'er I passed her; but who passed without
Much the same smile? This grew; I gave commands;
Then all smiles stopped together. There she stands
As if alive. Will't please you rise? We'll meet
The company below, then. I repeat,
The Count your Master's known munificence
Is ample warrant that no just pretence
Of mine for dowry will be disallowed;
Though his fair daughter's self, as I avowed
At starting, is my object. Nay, we'll go
Together down, Sir! Notice Neptune, though,
Taming a sea-horse, thought a rarity,
Which Claus of Innsbruck cast in bronze for me.

When the term *character* is used not to refer to a person in a literary work but to what he is like, it generally refers to his *whole* nature—his personality, his attitude toward life, his "spiritual" qualities, his intelligence, even his physical build, as well as his moral attributes.

CHARACTERIZATION

When we describe the nature of characters, we deal with the concept of characterization. How do we know what these characters are like? We simply examine the evidence in the particular work. We clearly do not formulate our idea of what a duke would be like and then try to force that image into Browning's poem; that procedure would make us guilty of what is sometimes called the "personal response," that is, deciding what a writer should say and then trying to "interpret" his work so that he seems to say it. No;

to perceive the character of Browning's Duke we must look at the evidence that Browning gives us in the poem and draw the conclusions from that evidence.

Just as we learn what our friends and acquaintances are like by seeing them and listening to them, and by hearing what others think of them, so we learn about the characters in imaginative literature. The only difference is that in a literary work we are given the evidence by the author, who understands his characters much better than we can understand people in real life, and who presents the evidence so as to direct our attention to his conception of the characters. His decision about what techniques of characterization to use will depend on such things as the point of view he adopts and the tone he wishes to establish; these concepts we shall discuss later.

A number of methods of characterization may be used in stories, poems, and plays. A person's nature may be revealed by what he says and does and by the clothes, the house and furnishings, and the friends he chooses. As in real life, we can see what a fictional character is like from his actions, his speech, his physical appearance, and his environment; in addition, we can see what he is like from what others say about him and from how they behave toward him.

Suppose, for example, we read at the beginning of a story:

The Cadillac swept up the tree-lined drive until, a half a mile from the road, it stopped before the marble steps of the white Georgian mansion. The chauffeur got out and hurried around to open the door for his employer, Mrs. Wilson Dubiel Abercrombie. The butler appeared from the front door to take Mrs. Abercrombie's glossy hat-box as she emerged from the car. Just before entering the mansion, Mrs. Abercrombie paused, flicked a speck of dust off a spotless white cuff, turned slightly and said coldly:

"I'll require your services again in an hour, Benson, and I'll expect you to have the car polished by then. It looks dirty."

The butler, after Mrs. Abercrombie had disappeared, glanced at Benson and shrugged his shoulders, as the chauffeur's lips silently began to form the words, "The b . . . ."

This episode offers for our observation many details about Mrs. Abercrombie's character; all we have to do is to look and listen and to form our conclusions. In this instance, the writer has relied on suggestion to let us know what the character is like.

The writer could also characterize Mrs. Abercrombie directly by telling us explicitly that she is rich and inconsiderate, among other things. Since the writer invented Mrs. Abercrombie and therefore knows her well, he could summarize for us the traits that we can perceive in the episode above, or add to them. Furthermore, the author could also tell us what Benson and the butler are thinking, for he knows them well, too. He could tell us that the butler was thinking resentfully, yet with resignation, of what Mrs. Abercrombie had said when he had asked for the afternoon off to visit his daughter in the hospital. In other words, some of our sources of information about characters in imaginative literature would not be available to us in real life.

MOTIVATION

Once we perceive the nature of a character in a given work, and indeed while we are in the actual process of perceiving it, we become concerned with the problem of motivation. If the character is involved in action of any kind, and especially if he is at all responsible for an event, we must consider whether his behavior is consistent with his character. Is Shakespeare's character Macbeth the kind of person who could kill the king, Duncan, as he does? Is that action consistent with his character as we perceive it especially in the earlier part of the play; is his ambition great enough; is he decisive enough? We are asking if this character is "well motivated" or if the action is well motivated.

We must be careful not to base our assessment of the motivation on too abstract a concept of what people generally do. We must consider what the particular character in the given work is like, for he may be quite different from most people even of his own kind.

Browning's Duke is not like most people, nor like most dukes. He is prouder and more ruthless, as we can see from his saying, "I choose / Never to stoop . . . ," and from the general violence of the time and place identified as the setting—Ferrara, Italy, in the sixteenth century. In assessing motivation, we may also have to take into account the circumstances, the provocations that affect the character: Macbeth may not have been a natural-born murderer, but he is greatly affected by the witches' predictions about his future eminence and by his wife's urgings to make that eminence possible.

Motivation sometimes raises difficult problems. On the one hand, a thoroughly well-motivated play or story may have the inevitability of fate, or it may seem trite (for example, in the old familiar stories about the love of a boy for the girl next door the motivation generated by the situation is so usual that it has become trite). On the other hand, unmotivated action can seem simply whimsical, or it can provide an extra dimension to the story. In Poe's "A Cask of Amontillado," Montresor's decision to murder Fortunato is evidently unmotivated. Knowing little about Montresor to begin with, we are told only that Fortunato had injured and then insulted him; such an abstract explanation offers little justification for the killing. But that apparent weakness of motivation is important here, because it shows us just how irrational and ruthless Montresor is, and makes the atmosphere of the story that much more horrifying. In this instance, the character is motivated more by his irrational and ruthless nature than by the actions of Fortunato.

PROTAGONIST AND ANTAGONIST

When we examine the characters in a work of fiction we inevitably and properly pay more attention to the main characters than to the minor ones. In reading Melville's novel *Moby-Dick,* a story about Captain Ahab's sailing his whaling ship in an almost insanely intense pursuit of the white whale, we concern ourselves much more with Ahab than with the harpooner Tashtego, for instance, for the captain is one of the main centers around which the story revolves. Ahab, that is, is the protagonist; his principal opponent, the white whale, is the antagonist.

Even if he does not always actively initiate the events, the protagonist is always the focal point of the action of a story, the character that the story is most obviously about. He is usually in the forefront of the action, and usually has the most to say, whether we like or approve of him or not. Macbeth is clearly the protagonist in his play even though he is scarcely admirable; he often shares our attention with Lady Macbeth, but we know that the play is not primarily about her. Nor is she the antagonist, for she is aligned with her husband, despite their differences. The antagonist is the main person or thing or force that opposes the protagonist; in *Macbeth,* there are several antagonists: Macduff, Fleance, and the other Scots who finally bring Macbeth down.

The situation in many stories is too complicated and subtle to be resolved into the opposition of a single hero and a single villain. The antagonist may be not a person, but a nonhuman thing like the whale in *Moby-Dick,* or a disembodied force, like fate or the gods in Sophocles' tragedy *Oedipus Rex* (in which a king of ancient Greece discovers that he has not succeeded in defying the oracles' predictions about the course of his life). At the same time, if there is a single person who embodies or represents or is the particular instrument of a general force which is the fundamental opposition to the protagonist, that person is the antagonist. What he represents should be clearly noted; we should learn to distinguish between the ostensible and the real, or the overt and the implicit antagonists. The protagonist also is sometimes a thing or a force: some critics have identified the protagonist in *The Return of the Native* as the heath, the wild and desolate countryside that is the setting of Thomas Hardy's novel. Again, the protagonist is not always the winner, nor do we necessarily want him to win; in some detective stories, a murderer is the protagonist. And, as we have seen, there may be more than one protagonist or antagonist. The basic point is that if there is a representative of one side of the main conflict who serves as the center of the story, he is designated the protagonist, and his opponent the antagonist.

Thus far, we have touched on only the fundamental concepts relative to character. Our next step is to examine some of their subtleties and refinements.

SUBTLETIES AND REFINEMENTS

SPECIAL PROBLEMS OF INTERPRETATION

Some of the problems in the interpretation of characterization and in the analysis of characters will also arise later in relation to other literary concepts, but we shall begin investigating the central issues now.

The personal response. The personal response stems from our natural tendency to think of everything in terms of ourselves, individually, and to feel that only that which we ourselves think and feel is truly valid. On this basis, we tend to see in a story, poem, or play only what we individually have experienced. If we are not careful, we can find ourselves in a completely untenable position. In the motion picture *Never on Sunday* a young woman in Greece ascribes the most improbably beneficent motives and emotions to Euripides' Medea, who is one of the most cruel and vicious women ever to appear in a play; the young woman was projecting her own feelings and attitudes into the character on the stage. We must remember that not everyone is like us and that our own experiences are not all-inclusive. If we remember this, we will see how Shakespeare's Othello can be basically kind and noble and yet kill his wife Desdemona out of jealousy, or how Oedipus can insist on finding out the whole truth—that without realizing it he fulfilled a prophesy by killing his father and marrying his mother—even after he realizes that the truth is horrible. We must recognize that an author rarely writes just what we would write.

The stock response. A second general problem is that of the "stock response," which is allied to the "personal response" but has a broader basis. The "stock response" is that of the reader who interprets the characters in imaginative literature according to the attitudes and beliefs most conventional in his society. To him, a mother is always kind and devoted, the moon is always beautiful, a dog is always man's best friend. The "stock response" conceives of only relatively trite, unexceptional characterization.

Let us look again briefly at *Macbeth* and *Oedipus* to see how a stock response can falsify the interpretation of character. In both cases, the protagonist can be absolved of responsibility for his deeds if our response to the events in the play is too conventional: Macbeth is ambitious, of course, but ambition is a good thing, and it isn't really his fault that it leads to murder, for his wife pushed him into it. Similarly, Oedipus doesn't deserve to be punished for what he did, for he didn't know he was doing wrong, and anyway, fate made him do it. We should not think of Macbeth simply as a henpecked husband nor of Oedipus as the victim of a practical joke.

GENERAL PROBLEMS OF INTERPRETATION

If we are on guard against the "personal" and the "stock" response, we can deal more satisfactorily with the other, more specific problems and subtleties of characterization. When a writer tells us directly what his characters are like, we have relatively few problems; when he does not, but instead makes us judge for ourselves from the evidence he provides, we have to take special pains to assess accurately the validity and significance of the evidence.

Ambiguous evidence. In plays and motion pictures, the visible action and the setting are often main sources of information about the characters: if we see a man in a back street draw a switchblade knife, stab a nicely dressed girl, and run off with her purse, we can form some conclusions about his nature without difficulty. What is clearly visible and unambiguous is not likely to be misinterpreted. Yet what is clearly visible can sometimes be ambiguous. In the ballad "Sir Patrick Spens," for example, the protagonist laughs when he receives a letter from the king ordering him to sea at a very bad time of year; at first it is hard to tell whether Sir Patrick is carefree and confident, sardonically or despairingly amused, or simply dismayed by what he reads.

We must be even more careful in interpreting those evidences of character that we receive secondhand. When Browning's Duke talks about his last Duchess, he provides us with a certain insight into her character—but how much can we believe him? The information he provides is not complete, and his understanding of her is not very reliable not only because he has a message to convey (he wants to indicate how his future Duchess should *not* behave), but also because of the effect his own character has on his judgment.

Similarly, we must allow for a character's personal bias when he talks or even thinks about himself. No one, in literature or in real life, knows himself thoroughly, and no matter how he describes his own nature, that description will be affected by the very nature of the speaker. The Duke in "My Last Duchess" tells the truth about his character when he says "I choose / Never to stoop"; to him this attitude is perfectly proper and natural—his overweening pride would take it to be so—but our reaction would differ.

The consistency principle. There is a solution to the dilemma evident above, a difficult but necessary venture to undertake. We must correlate and cross-check the evidence from all the various sources in the given work. We must try to insure the consistency of our interpretation of a character by determining whether the inference we have drawn from a certain action or a speech, for instance, is reconcilable with that drawn perhaps from the character's clothing and environment. Often we can perceive a dominant characteristic in a given character, such as pride or egoism in

Browning's Duke, on which we can focus our correlation. Not that we can do so mechanically, for a character may be complex and full of normal human inconsistencies, but we can assume that in good writing these inconsistencies are not likely to be improbable. We can assume, in other words, that a writer will try to make his characters seem basically consistent and his possibilities seem probable.

To illustrate this correlating of evidence, let us consider "My Last Duchess" again. How are we to interpret the words "I gave commands; / Then all smiles stopped together. There she stands / As if alive"? Is it more consistent with the Duke's character as we perceive it in the rest of the poem to infer that he divorced his last Duchess, or that he sent her to a convent (and that she later died), or that he had her killed? The collocation of "all smiles stopped" and "as if alive" would seem to indicate that he had her killed, and the other aspects of the poem that we have noted earlier would support this interpretation.

This discussion of what we may call the consistency principle perhaps seems to suggest that there is only one right way to interpret a given character, or anything else, in a literary work; that the author must have meant one thing, and that we must find and stick to his one interpretation. This suggestion is partly true and partly false. Briefly, we can assume that an author does have some idea in mind which is reflected in the various facets of his work. Yet we cannot identify it so positively that we refuse to allow any other interpretation, for two principal reasons. First, we can never be sure what the author's intention was. Even if we ask him, as we sometimes can if he is still living, we may find that he will not or cannot tell us exactly what he had in mind; most authors' creative work is just as susceptible to the influence of the subconscious as anyone else's. Alternately, it is risky to rely exclusively on our own interpretation of his work to reveal the author's intention, as the variety of interpretations of almost any given work demonstrates; many very different accounts of *Hamlet* have been advanced as the one that Shakespeare really meant. Second, the fact that amid the variety of interpretations there are many equally satisfying to discriminating readers indicates that we should be receptive to inferences that differ from our own, as long as they are justifiable on the basis of the work itself.

We should consider valid any interpretation of a character that makes sense in the light of everything else in the work. Applied conscientiously, this rule of thumb will help us avoid the problems inherent in the so-called "intentional fallacy"—that is, judging the intent and success of a work of art by *our* idea of the author's intention. At the same time, however, we must apply it sensibly: we should maintain a common-sense standard of probability when we search for consistency, and we should be reasonable in searching out inconsistencies. So that we will not limit our conception of a literary work too much, or miss important points, we should remember that consistency often exists on several different levels. In Robert Frost's "Stopping by Woods on a Snowy Evening," the speaker's feeling about the woods is one of satisfaction with a quiet and beautiful scene, and, on another level, a death wish:

> The woods are lovely, dark and deep.
> But I have promises to keep,
> And miles to go before I sleep. . . .

Both interpretations are consistent, on different levels, with what we know about the speaker from the rest of the poem.

Changes in character. Our consistency principle will help us deal with yet another problem in the analysis of character. That problem is the one created by a real or an apparent change in a character.

Let us first consider the real change that occurs in Othello. At the beginning of Shakespeare's play he is gentle, noble, and very much in love with Desdemona—he marries her for love, and receives the blessing of her father, a senator, and of the Duke of Venice. By Act V, however, Othello smothers his wife, having be-

come bitterly jealous and suspicious, as his speeches to her in Act
IV, scene 2, show:

> *Othello:*   O thou weed,
> Who art so lovely fair, and smell'st so sweet,
> That the sense aches at thee, would thou hadst ne'er been born!

> *Desdemona:* Alas, what ignorant sin have I committed?

> *Othello:* Was this fair paper, this most goodly book,
> Made to write 'whore' upon? What committed? . . .
> Heaven stops the nose at it, and the moon winks;
> The bawdy wind, that kisses all it meets,
> Is hush'd within the hollow mine of earth
> And will not hear it. What committed?
> Impudent strumpet!

(ll. 67–73, 77–81)

This obvious change naturally raises a question of motivation
that falls into two parts: is Othello's character the kind to change,
and if so, is the change the kind that would be likely to occur? To
answer the first part of the question, we have to consider Othello's
character as it appears at the beginning of the play, and also the
provocation that he is given. To answer the second part, we must
use the consistency principle: the question becomes "Is the suspi-
ciousness, violence, and disgust that Othello reveals toward the
end of the play consistent with the honest, trusting, and loving
character we find in him earlier?" If the answer is "yes," Othello's
character has not changed so radically that we no longer recognize
it, but has simply developed along probable lines. If our answer is
"no," the work is either badly written, or purposely inconsistent
(like Dr. Jekyll and Mr. Hyde, in Stevenson's story), or we have
missed something in the work and must reconsider it more carefully. In Shakespeare's play, the answer to the question is "yes," and
the change in Othello's behavior is consistent with his general
character: a simple and noble man, he has been persuaded by a
man he believed to be equally straightforward that his beloved wife

has been unfaithful. His disillusionment made him incensed with
Desdemona's apparent hypocrisy and prompted him to destroy
what seemed so loving and fair, yet was evidently so corrupt—and
so destructive of others, like himself.

Next, let us consider a change that may be more apparent than
real. About halfway through Hemingway's short story "The Short
Happy Life of Francis Macomber," it becomes evident that Macomber's wife spends the night with Wilson, the hunter who is con-
ducting the Macombers' African safari. Before this episode Wilson
has demonstrated his toughness and integrity, and a certain sympathy and even liking for Macomber. Does Wilson step out of character by making love to Mrs. Macomber, or does that episode
merely reveal another element in Wilson or show another way in
which his character is manifested? When we consider the nature of
Wilson's integrity, we find that he has a strict and honorable code
of behavior, but that it applies only to hunting and to the treatment
of the animals; otherwise, he is "realistic." He would not seek out
Mrs. Macomber, but he is willing to accept her advances. This
kind of new development in a character appears frequently in literary works, especially near the beginning. A similar case occurs in
Macbeth. We learn in the opening scenes that the protagonist is a
brave and ambitious warrior and nobleman; in battle, we are told,

> . . . brave Macbeth (well he deserves that name),
> Disdaining Fortune, with his brandish'd steel,
> Which smok'd with bloody execution
> (Like valour's minion), carv'd out his passage. . . .
>
> (Act I, scene 2, ll. 16–19)

Soon, however, we learn that Macbeth is at least partly dominated
by his wife; this is implied when she addresses her thoughts to her
absent husband in Act I, scene 5:

> Hie thee hither,
> That I may pour my spirits in thine ear
> And chastise with the valour of my tongue
> All that impedes thee. . . .
>
> (ll. 26–29)

Is this likely? One would hardly think so, in the abstract; but we cannot deal with character in the abstract. As a preliminary step, we must realize that our knowledge of human character is not complete, and then admit that if we knew more about psychology we would find no real inconsistency in Macbeth or Wilson. Next, we must look at the works themselves, and observe the particular shades and nuances of character that the authors have given Macbeth and Wilson. We will conclude that they are sufficiently different from most men of their kinds to behave as they do; we cannot expect all characters to run true to type. Last, when we gain a new insight or see a new manifestation of a man's character, we should ask if it is consistent with what we already know.

Minor characteristics. Some traits and physical qualities are designed merely to make a character lifelike, especially in a novel, and although these qualities may sometimes be mildly inconsistent with the character's apparently basic nature, we need not let this bother us. When we see in Faulkner's *Intruder in the Dust* that Lucas, the stiff-necked old colored man who is accused of murder, likes gingersnaps, we may even feel that the very peculiarity of this trait makes him more believable.

A writer may also give a character certain traits to make him likeable or unpleasant. A hero's clean-cut features and a traditional villain's greasy black mustache are so designed. We should note these traits being careful not to let the character's other traits blind us to them. We should be especially sure to note attractive or unattractive traits if the character otherwise presents a different impression; if a girl in a story is attractive except that she perspires heavily, we must take that trait into our account of her nature, for it is a significant exception to the rule. In the common case of characters who are neither thoroughly good nor thoroughly bad, we will have to register both kinds of traits and correlate them sensibly. For instance, how are we to feel about tragic heroes, such as Othello or Macbeth? The traits they display lead us to admire them for what they have been, or might have been, but to condemn them for what they have become; the two impressions are not basically inconsistent. In addition, to guard against a personal response, we must correlate our feelings about a character with the traits and the behavior he manifests: do we like a certain character because he is actually presented as likeable, or simply because we happen to like that kind of person? The English Romantic poet Shelley felt that Satan was the real hero of Milton's epic of the fall of man, *Paradise Lost,* because he was a rebel against the "tyranny" of God. But Satan is clearly the arch-villain; Shelley's impressions were colored by the fact that he was very much a rebel himself.

CATEGORIES OF CHARACTER

As we analyze the characters in imaginative writing, we will come to see that they fall into certain categories that help us either to systematize our knowledge of particular works or clarify the general nature of character and characterization. Some of these categorical concepts, such as "protagonist" and "antagonist," which we have already discussed, are related to the position or function of the character in the work; others help define the nature or extent of the characterization.

Nature or extent categories. This class consists of such concepts as the stock character, the type or the individual, the static or the developing character, the real or the "cardboard" character, and the flat or the round character.

A stock character is a literary type character, one that has appeared and reappeared in imaginative literature so often that we all know exactly what he is like: the villain with the handle-bar mustache, the city slicker, the boy who is always getting into trouble. Most stock characters have some basis in reality, but they are exaggerations in the first place, and their nature has been crystallized artifically in literature. Glaring examples of stock characters are hard to find in good literature, particularly as major figures. More often they occupy such places as that of the grave-digger in

Hamlet, a recognizable "irreverent servant" of the same type as Juliet's nurse (and as Hazel, in cartoons and on television); these examples show that stock characters are not necessarily to be condemned, especially when the author adds something to the traditional ingredients of the type.

Though a stock character is a literary type, we use the general term "type character" for one derived primarily from real life. We have all known people who are uncertain of themselves and try to display a sophistication and even a cynicism that will protect them. This type, with variations, occurs in real life, and an author may reproduce one in his work. Holden Caulfield, the teen-aged protagonist and narrator of J. D. Salinger's *Catcher in the Rye,* is basically just such a type, though that is not all he is. A pure type character is seldom found in an important position in realistic literature simply because good fictional characters are based on real human beings, who do not adhere all of the time to all of the same characteristics and therefore cannot be typed. Similarly, completely individual people are almost never found in real life or in realistic literature, for we all have a few characteristics in common. The question to ask ourselves about a given character is, "How individual, or original, is he, and how typical is he?"

The second set of contrasting categories is that of the static and the developing characters. The meanings of the terms are self-evident. In many novels and plays, the character of the main figure does not remain the same from beginning to end, but is modified by the events he takes part in, although the minor characters may remain relatively unaffected. We have already noted the important changes that take place in Othello; similarly, Raskolnikov, the protagonist of Dostoievski's *Crime and Punishment,* changes from a cold-blooded murderer to a warm human being capable of sincere repentance—this change is the main feature of the novel. We should note that these are relatively long works; it usually takes some time for a writer to work out a character change or development, for a person's nature usually changes only gradually. A

genuine change or new development in a person's character comes
about suddenly only when he has been profoundly and radically
affected by some experience or has reached the point at which the
cumulative effect of a long series of experiences affects him, and it
takes a very competent writer indeed to present such crises believ-
ably and effectively. Most characters in short narratives are therefore static, though not for that reason badly drawn.

A value judgment is usually implied in the next dichotomy, that
between real and "cardboard" characters. Real characters are
those who have vitality: they are alive, and seem to be made of
flesh and blood, of mind, heart, and soul, and almost exist independently of the author. In his play entitled *Six Characters in Search
of an Author,* the Italian Luigi Pirandello deliberately explores the
idea of the independent existence of the characters. As the title
suggests, the six characters appear as practically real people who
are involved in a series of events and who are impelled to reveal
them; they approach the stage from the audience at the beginning
of the play, demanding to be heard. This is an extreme case, however; usually, we call those characters real who simply seem to
have a good deal of vitality. Note that this distinction between real
and cardboard is not exactly the same as that between realistic and
unrealistic characters. There, the question is whether one sees such
people in real life or not, whereas our present distinction is concerned only with the vitality of the character in the context of the
particular work. Many of Dickens' minor characters are quite unrealistic caricatures but have tremendous vitality, while a poor
writer may present a recognizably real type of person but fail to
"bring him to life" in his work.

It is difficult to say exactly what makes a character real. A stock
character will be mechanical; too typic or too eccentric a character
will also be artificial, animated by push-button rather than any
"life-force." Again, a character's vitality or "reality" may depend
partly on how well the author depicts the minor gestures and small

talk by which we can judge whether or not a person is alive. At the
same time, the vitality of a character is a relative matter; none is
completely cardboard nor completely real, for all are partly the
creation of the author, reflecting to some degree his experience
with real life and human beings.

The last two varieties of characterization are the flat and the
round.[1] A flat character is one who has one characteristic and one
only; Forster cites Dickens' characters, with the possible exception
of Pip, in *Great Expectations,* and of David Copperfield. Poe's
Montresor, too, is almost nothing but revenge personified. Flat
characters are types or caricatures, as Forster says, while round
characters have the variety and inconsistency of traits that make
people human. A truly flat character's behavior is always obviously
consistent with his single trait; a round character can sometimes
surprise us, at least for the moment. We can never confidently pre-
dict the behavior of Hamlet or of Huckleberry Finn.

These two categories of characters overlap with some of the
others. A stock character, or highly typic or eccentric character, is
a flat character, while a mixture of the two elements produces a
rounder one. A round character is almost inevitably real or vital;
conversely a flat one tends to be cardboard, but we have only to
think of Dickens' people and of Montresor to realize that a really
vital writer can make some flat characters live.

It should be clear that flat characterization is not necessarily bad
and round characterization good. While round characters are fundamentally more interesting than flat ones, each kind has its place
and function. As minor characters in a novel, for instance, flat
characters are invaluable as a frame of reference for the protagonist: the scores of minor characters in Dickens' novels are a case in
point. And in a highly symbolic or allegorical work many of the
principal characters themselves have to be flat if they are to be
broadly representative: in Edmund Spenser's great allegory of the

[1] See E. M. Forster, *Aspects of the Novel,* New York, 1927, pp. 103–118.

sixteenth century, *The Faerie Queene,* almost all the characters stand for specific qualities like hypocrisy or holiness and can hardly be anything but flat.

Position or function of characters. In discussing how these varieties of character could be effectively used, we begin to consider further the literary concepts related to characters' functions in imaginative writing.

The concepts of the protagonist and the antagonist, though simple enough basically, are sometimes more complex in actual application. The protagonist or antagonist may be not a person, but a force or a thing, like Hardy's heath. Again the protagonist may be multiple: both the young lovers are protagonists in *Romeo and Juliet.* Furthermore, the protagonist and antagonist may be intermixed in one way or another. In "Dr. Jekyll and Mr. Hyde," the protagonist turns into the antagonist by drinking a fiendish potion that changes both his appearance and his nature. Similarly, if we take the conflict in *Hamlet* to be between the resolute and the vacillating sides of the prince's nature, then the protagonist and the antagonist are again the same person; as Hamlet himself describes the conflict in his mind, "the native hue of resolution / Is sicklied o'er with the pale cast of thought." Finally, we must remember those cases in which our identification of the protagonist or antagonist changes as we proceed through the narrative. Shelley's calling Satan the hero of *Paradise Lost* is based on the fact that Satan occupies the center of the stage and initiates the action in the first two Books of the epic; but the perspective changes later, and this, Shelley chose perversely to overlook.

The protagonist and antagonist are main or major characters in a work. More liberally and sensibly, however, especially in long works, we include as main characters those other figures who have a good deal of influence on the protagonist and antagonist, or are integrally and importantly involved in the central action. In discussing *Oedipus,* for example, we have to consider Jocasta, Oedipus' mother and wife, a major character, for although the play is not her story she is almost continually on stage, encouraging the king's search in her ignorance or attempting to dissuade him from it when she forsees the outcome. To draw the line between major and minor characters we judge how deeply a given character is involved in the main action.

The main characters are the most important ones in terms of the plot, yet there are certain kinds of minor characters who, though sometimes not really involved with the action at all, are nevertheless very important to the characterization of a major character, to the development of the plot, or even to the tone and the implied significance of the whole work.

One of these is the "foil character," who serves to clarify and emphasize by contrast another, usually a major, figure. The foil character's nature will be in some important respect diametrically opposed to the character he sets off, as the straightforwardness and comparative simplemindedness of Hamlet's friend Horatio sets off by contrast the prince's complex and subtle mind. Almost always the antagonist and protagonist serve as foils to each other, as Montresor's cruel cunning and Fortunato's good-natured stupidity contrast neatly in "A Cask of Amontillado," but we usually reserve the term foil-character for one who is more important as a means of clarifying and emphasizing another character than for his function in the plot.

Another, more significant minor character is exemplified by the Fool in *King Lear*. He is a "chorus character," so called because of the similarity of his function to that of the chorus in Greek tragedy; he is an interested and articulate spectator to the action, although he directly affects it little if at all. The Fool in *Lear* stands by the king but does not influence the course of the action directly; for the most part he half sympathizes with, half mocks Lear's plight through his general attitude and his remarks. He sees and understands more than the other characters in the play; he reflects the perspective of the author and of the audience, who recognize the tragedy resulting from Lear's foolish and proud actions while

realizing that the king brought his troubles on himself by that foolishness.

In prose and verse narrative, we seldom find a chorus character,
principally because his function there can be fulfilled to some extent by the author's "point of view." We will discuss this concept
later, but we must consider the fact that many stories are told not
by a supposedly omniscient author writing in the third person, but
by one of the characters connected directly or indirectly with the
actions described. Thus some characters in imaginative literature
as narrators embody the perspective from which the events are
seen. Ishmael, the narrator of *Moby-Dick,* is such a character; he
signs aboard Ahab's ship and stays with it until it is finally destroyed, taking part in the action but always preserving a somewhat broader perspective than the rest of the sailors. Since he is
independent of the moral problems of the novel (though some critics do not take this view), his position is closely analogous to that
of the chorus character in drama. Huckleberry Finn, on the other
hand, in telling his own story, not only provides the point of view
but serves as the protagonist as well, and cannot be considered a
chorus character.

The "point of view" in a literary work, as we shall see, is one of
the most important concerns of the critical reader. A narrator,
therefore, has to be considered carefully, for his own nature and
his relationship with the other characters and their actions actually
define the point of view: for example, if we fail to define clearly
the Duke's character in "My Last Duchess," we will certainly miss
the point of the poem.

Because we do not want to miss the point of poems, plays, or
stories, we start our critical analyses with the characters. They are
the core of the content, the basic subject matter, because literature
is written by and for human beings. We must be able to understand
the characters and their relationships in a literary work on a sophisticated level in order to deal with literature intelligently. For
this, we need all our perspicuity and a thorough familiarity with
the elements and basic techniques of characterization.

Narrative

BASIC TERMS AND CONCEPTS

NARRATIVE

A narrative recounts an event or series of events in any form or medium, prose or verse, dramatic or nondramatic. It is one kind of literary approach, different from the approaches of description, exposition, and argumentation, though these various kinds of discourse are usually mixed, especially in extended works.

We should distinguish clearly between these approaches for at least two reasons. First, we may learn a great deal about the construction and the flavor of a literary work by observing within it the proportions of the various forms of discourse. One of the notable features of the structure of *Moby-Dick,* for instance, is the number of expository chapters on whaling it includes among the more strictly narrative ones. And some of the basic differences between Hemingway's short stories and Conrad's are due to the larger proportion of description and exposition in the latter. A second and more important reason for our distinction is that our analytical approach will vary according to the type of discourse. We do not look for the same kind of structure or technique in *Paradise Lost* and Pope's *Essay on Man;* they are both poetic works on the subject of man's place in the universe, but the first tells the story of the revolt in Heaven of Satan and his cohorts and of "Man's first disobedience," while the other is a series of abstract and expository verse essays. We shall concern ourselves now with the techniques and concepts related primarily to narrative.

PLOT

One basic concept of narrative is plot. A plot is based on a series of events that are all partly the result of some continuing cause. Many people inaccurately assume that plot is inherent in narrative, but a narrative may tell of a series of events that are related only chronologically or perhaps locally. That is, they may have happened one after the other, like the events of a small boy's day, or they may all have happened in the same place. Such narratives are not plotted, for a plot is formed by a causal sequence of events. The plot begins when the continuing cause begins, and that cause carries the sequence forward. At the same time, single events in the series are often the cause of later ones; in *Oedipus,* for instance, the unwillingness of the prophet Tiresias to reveal the whole horrible truth makes the suspicious king think that Tiresias and perhaps others are plotting against him. Oedipus consequently has little faith in what the prophet says. The principal continuing cause, Oedipus' desire for knowledge of past happenings, is in operation at the same time, and it leads eventually to the conclusion of the particular series of events that forms the plot of the play.

A plot, in addition, is a sequence of events that constitutes a whole unit separate from the happenings that precede or follow it.

Thus *Oedipus* begins with the plague, not with Oedipus' birth, and it ends with Oedipus' ruin without tracing the subsequent events of his life. Similarly, Poe chose to limit the plot of "A Cask of Amontillado" to the unit formed by Montresor's murder of Fortunato; if he had elected to include in the story the events that constituted the "thousand injuries" and the "insult" that Montresor felt he had suffered, the plot and the whole effect of the narrative would have been different from those of the particular short story he actually wrote. Since an author includes in his story only those events and bits of information which aid his chosen structure and strengthen his particular focus, we can better understand that structure and focus by noting what the author omitted as well as what he included.

CONFLICT

Finally, in order to constitute a whole unit, a plot must have a certain pattern to it—a beginning, a middle, and an end, as Aristotle stated in his *Poetics*. It begins with the activation of a conflict, develops that conflict, and ends with its resolution. In defining plot as a causal sequence of events we specified that a principal continuing cause or motive determines at least partly the events and the sequence they compose. It is possible for a narrative to be a causal sequence with a continuing cause without being plotted (for example, the growth of a tree); a story is not said to be plotted unless that cause stems from a conflict which is worked out deliberately in the story. The principal cause, that is, resides in the conflict that is the basis of the plot. The term "conflict" is familiar; it is the result of an opposition between at least two sides. Just as it takes two to make an argument, it takes two opposing people or forces to produce the conflict basic to a plot. Without this opposition there is no conflict, and without a conflict there is no plot. The conflict may be overt and violent, or implicit and subdued; it may be visible in action, or it may take place entirely in a character's mind; it may exist in different and sometimes contrasting forms, and on different levels of meaning; but by definition it is inherent in the concept of plot.

Let us illustrate. The conflict between Macbeth's ambition and the opposing characters and forces is overt and violent: the play is punctuated with murders and battles. The conflict between Walter Mitty (in James Thurber's "Secret Life of Walter Mitty") and his drab and henpecked existence, on the other hand, is subdued and internal: the story is a series of Walter's daydreams of heroism in action. And Ernest Hemingway's famous short novel, *The Old Man and the Sea,* is on one level an account of the conflict between a man and the sea and the fish, but on a deeper level the conflict is between man's need and desire to achieve something greater than the ordinary, and the natural and human forces that oppose the endeavor.

RESOLUTION

Once the basic conflict in a narrative is activated, the opposing forces work against each other, developing the conflict until its resolution. Like all conflicts, it may be resolved in favor of the protagonist or the antagonist, or in a draw, or a temporary suspension of hostilities; but it is resolved somehow. The resolution, then, is the end of the conflict in a particular plot: Macbeth's death in battle, the sinking of Ahab's ship, the revelation of the whole truth of Oedipus' past. Yet the story may continue past the resolution of the plot into a "denouement" (un-knotting), for a writer may feel it necessary to deal with certain after effects of the conflict and its resolution in order to conclude the plot effectively: *Hamlet* ends with Horatio's valediction and the arrival of the Swedish prince Fortinbras, who is to assume control of Denmark; and *Oedipus* ends with the king's blinding himself and his farewell to his daughters.

SETTING

Now, with the addition of one more concept we will have discussed all the basic elements of the subject matter of narrative:
characters, action (the events of the narrative), and setting. Obviously, the actions of the characters take place at some time, in
some place, amid some things; these temporal and spatial sur-
roundings are the setting. Even if a story took place in a timeless
void, that void would be the setting, a striking one at that.

There is a great variety of possible settings, and of relationships
between the settings and the characters and action. We need not
discuss the various settings writers may choose. What concerns us
here is the possible relationships between the setting and the other
elements of the narrative, for those relationships make the choice
of setting crucial. The setting may be slight, vague, and sparsely
detailed, or full and sharply detailed, but in either case it can be
important in the story, for either or both of two reasons: for the verisimilitude it can lend to the story, and the positive contribution it
can make to its nature and effect.

By verisimilitude we mean the appearance of truth or reality,
the impression that the events of the story could happen. This
impression is created partly by small physical details such as the
ropes and spars of the ship in *Moby-Dick,* and it also depends on a
large and dominant physical element like the London of George
Orwell's *1984,* which differs so much from present-day London
(there are skyscrapers everywhere and two-way television sets in
every room) that new and strange events seem probable.

When we point out the effect of the novelty and strangeness of
the setting in Orwell's book, we are indicating one way in which
the setting can do more for a story than merely make it seem likely. A setting can create an atmosphere that will help produce the
particular quality and effect of the story. Emily Brontë's *Wuther-*

ing Heights owes much of its particular effect to the pervasive atmosphere of wildness and eerieness produced by the moors that are its setting. And Poe is famous for the creation of atmosphere in his short stories by means of setting, as in "The Masque of the Red Death" with its lurid decaying mansion.

Finally the setting can actually influence the course of events in the story by directly affecting the characters and by encouraging certain kinds of events while inhibiting others. In Conrad's *Heart of Darkness,* the savage and menacing African jungle exerts an almost overwhelming influence on the narrator, Marlow; and the Mississippi River, in *Huckleberry Finn,* certainly is a likely locale for adventurous variety, not for polite drawing-room comedy. We should not underestimate the power of the setting, for it can operate strongly in many different ways. It can even be a protagonist or antagonist, as is the heath in Hardy's *Return of the Native* and the country itself in *War and Peace,* Tolstoy's novel of the Napoleonic wars in Russia.

POINT OF VIEW

To understand imaginative narrative we must consider the author's "point of view" or angle of narration as well as the content of his work. This "point of view" is not the author's general attitude toward life or toward his story, but is a specific concept that we must understand clearly.

When we identify the point of view of a story, we identify the narrator. We ask, "Who is supposed to be telling this story?" The writer often pretends, so to speak, to be someone else. He may allow himself to have more knowledge and more kinds of knowledge than an ordinary man has, or he may pretend that he has less knowledge than he actually does or only certain kinds of knowledge. And sometimes he will pretend to be someone entirely different, presenting what knowledge he allows himself as if it were transmuted by the personality and emotions of that person.

For example, a writer cannot actually know at first hand what goes on in the mind of someone else, but in *Crime and Punishment* Dostoievski allows himself to read the protagonist Raskolnikov's mind and reveal to us what he is thinking and feeling. On the other hand, in his short story "The Killers," Hemingway tells us practically nothing about his characters' thoughts, refusing to allow himself that knowledge even though he could easily have done so since the characters are his own creations. Again, Poe was not an Italian nobleman named Montresor, but he wrote "A Cask of Amontillado" as if he were and presented Fortunato and the events that transpired as they would appear to the rather unsavory protagonist.

The many different points of view are all variations or combinations of certain basic types. First, almost all stories are written either in the third person or the first person. The writer may either look at the people and the events from the outside, not from among them, and refer to them as "he," "she," and "they"; or he may write as if he were a character connected with the subject matter of the narrative, saying "I saw this happen," "I heard him say . . . ," or "I did this."

The general effect of these two basic points of view differs. The third-person point of view provides a more dispassionate perspective on the characters and events, for they are not near and around the narrator but on a different plane. The writer is outside, looking in; he may see very far in, but his position is nevertheless outside. And the reader's position is therefore also outside, since he inevitably sees things as the writer describes them. The first-person point of view, on the other hand, involves the writer—and therefore the reader—in the subject matter of the narrative. The writer is vicariously "inside," no matter how far away he may be from the center of the action.

To clarify the difference between the third- and first-person points of view, let us consider Arthur Miller's *Death of a Salesman* and Melville's *Moby-Dick*. Miller's play is about an elderly traveling salesman, Willy Loman, who is trying desperately but in vain to preserve the fiction that he and his family are successful in the materialistic world that he believes—or thinks he believes—is the only important one. But he finally realizes that he himself is a failure, and his beloved son Biff rejects him and the values he tries to maintain, for Biff sees that his own shiftlessness and dishonesty are the result of his trying to measure up to his father's distorted sense of values. The only solution that Willy can find is suicide. Like almost all plays, this is presented from the third-person point of view, and no matter how sorry we feel for Willy Loman, no matter how closely we may identify ourselves with him, his wife, or his son, and realize that their troubles are like ours, we are not in their sphere; we see them from a distance and in a wider perspective than their own. In *Moby-Dick,* however, we adopt the point of view of Ishmael, who is a member of Ahab's crew, hunts whales, and sees the white whale destroy the captain. We are therefore closely involved in the events, no matter how foreign they are to our ordinary lives, for we are there, in the same sphere, vicariously. The effect of either point of view is valuable, depending on the nature of the subject matter and what the writer wants to make of it; it is up to us as critical readers to perceive what effect the particular point of view has on the subject matter of a given story.

Death of a Salesman is an extreme example of the third-person point of view because it is a play, and plays are written both from the "outside," from the third-person point of view, and also from a position that does not allow the narrator to see into the characters' minds directly. This is known as the "third-person, objective" point of view; it reports only what a camera and a tape-recorder register. Hemingway maintains this point of view in "The Killers" almost completely, for he shows us what his characters do and records what they say, but does not tell us what they are thinking or feeling. These thoughts and feelings we must infer from what they do and say. When one of them describes how he feels, we get the information not directly from an all-knowing author, but from a character whose words must be assessed in the light of his personality. We see the characters, actions, and setting of "The Killers" much as we see people and their behavior in daily life, strictly from the outside.

If Hemingway had elected to read his characters' minds, as Dickens did when writing *A Tale of Two Cities* and many of his other novels, we would have called his point of view "omniscient," which means "all-knowing." Dickens tells us much about what goes on in the minds and hearts of his characters. Note that he does not necessarily tell us all—that would be impossible and in fact undesirable; he limits his omniscience. Most writers who adopt the omniscient point of view modify it by restricting the depth of their insights or by limiting them to only certain characters. But we can assume that the inside information we get is reliable, for it comes to us directly from the creator of those thoughts and feelings and of the characters who experience them.

We classify the principal varieties of the first-person point of view according to the function of the narrator in the story. Thus, in "A Cask of Amontillado" and *Huckleberry Finn* the point of view is that of the protagonist. In the Sherlock Holmes stories we have the point of view of the detective's rather unintelligent friend, Watson, who sometimes has an important role in the action, though not as a protagonist, and sometimes is little more than a spectator to it. The "innocent eye" or naive point of view of "That Evening Sun," by William Faulkner, is that of a minor character who reports but does not fully understand what is happening around him. The events and persons in the story will make different impressions on the different characters, depending on how much they are involved in the action and on their personalities. The choice of one character rather than another to establish the point of view is therefore crucial for the writer and must be observed carefully by the reader.

The study of points of view and their effect in different narratives can be a very demanding exercise because the variations of the technique and its relation to the other narrative elements can be so subtle and complex. We will examine some of these subtleties and refinements later, and the process will be rewarding because of the importance of the point of view to the particular nature of a narrative.

SUBTLETIES AND REFINEMENTS

PLOT STRUCTURE

Our earlier discussion of plot was concerned with its basic nature, the characteristics that distinguish it from other series of events. We now need to pursue the analysis of plot further; but first, a word of warning and qualification: although all plots have some kind of basic pattern, few have exactly the same pattern, nor do all plotted narratives have the same *amount* of plot. Some stories are highly plotted and some are lightly plotted. That is, in some stories the chain of events is very important and often complicated, while in others the events are few and form a tenuous pattern. Detective stories tend to be highly plotted; the reader's interest is in what happens next and how the plot will resolve itself. Hemingway's short story "A Clean, Well-Lighted Place," on the other hand, is very lighted plotted: the focus is on what the characters think and feel as they sit in a café and talk until closing time. A highly plotted narrative may have both an intricate main plot, and subplots as well, chains of events—like those involving Hamlet and Ophelia—which are subsidiary to the main plot, though connected with it. A lightly plotted story almost never has a subplot, and may consist of a single simple episode; it may hardly seem to be a story in the traditional sense at all and may give rise to weighty arguments about whether it is a narrative or an essay. Let us stay away from this shadow line between the two literary forms, however, and return to the relatively conventional plot.

Before a story opens, or in its early pages, a situation exists in which a potential conflict can be perceived; when something happens to make that conflict actual, the plot begins. A plot, by definition, has a pattern that stems from a conflict, which begins at a point that we may call the "activating circumstance." Before the activating circumstance the potential conflict may be clearly perceptible, as it is in the strained relations between Hamlet and the king and queen in the second scene of Shakespeare's play, or it may be almost imperceptible except retrospectively after it is activated, as in *Macbeth*. But when it is activated by some circumstance—when the fuse is lit—it starts to develop. The development may be short or long, rapid or slow, depending on the strength with which the author has invested the opposing forces or persons, and on many other things; it ends, as we have seen, when the conflict is resolved.

It is usually clear at the end of a highly plotted story that the conflict has been resolved, especially if the protagonist and antagonist confront each other in a decisive scene such as the last one in *Macbeth*. In many cases, however, the resolution is complicated by occurring in different stages or on different levels. At the end of *Oedipus,* for instance, the conflict is resolved on one level when the whole truth is revealed, and on another when the king says goodbye to his daughters and is led off, blind and defeated. This last event can be considered the denouement following the resolution achieved when the truth is revealed; what is denouement on one level can be part of the resolution on another. In some plots the resolution occurs gradually in a series of crises, each one bringing the victory of one side closer; at the end, the conflict has been resolved through the accumulated effect of the crises.

The course of development is simple and clear for many conflicts, however. In "A Cask of Amontillado" the action leads quite directly to the event—Montresor's burying Fortunato alive—that constitutes the major crisis and the resolution as well. Other plots are more complex with shifts in the advantage from one opponent to the other, through equally clear in the final resolution. In *Hamlet* the prince is sometimes actively forwarding his plans for revenging his father's death and sometimes is frustrated by his own hesitation or by the machinations of the usurper King Claudius. This shifting back and forth is an important key to the plot of the play, yet the resolution is clear and can be located precisely in the final scene, when almost everyone is killed.

These shifts of advantage we may call crises or turning points; sometimes there are several, sometimes only one or none. If there are any, the last is important, for it often indicates the direction of the resolution. It may be one step in the resolution. Consider an all too conventional boy-and-girl story for a moment: the hero falls in love with a girl who seems to like him; then along comes a rival who seems to court her successfully; the rival turns out to be a cad; the girl, disillusioned, thinks all men are beasts; the hero proposes and she, realizing he is her hero, says "yes"; they are married. The shifts here are obvious, but the one that really counts is her saying "yes," for it is then that the outcome of the conflict is determined. The last turning point is the major one not because it is the last, but because it makes the outcome a foregone conclusion. In this kind of story true love triumphs; once true mutual love is established, the resolution has been set up and the outcome is determined.

The foregoing describes one common pattern of events, but there are many others.

First, the crucial turning point sometimes occurs early in the plot. In *Macbeth,* things start going against Macbeth when Fleance escapes to rally the opposition, an event that occurs in the middle of the play. The succeeding crises mitigate or intensify the established tendency without radically altering it; the outcome of the plot is thus predetermined by Fleance's escape.

Second, there may be but one turning point in which the advantage shifts from one side in the conflict to the other. Everything will go against the hero at first, but then the trend will change in a crucial episode and things will go his way from then on. Crises will occur—moments when the prevailing tendency is challenged—but no reversals, except for the major one.

Third, an advantage for one side may be established in the activating conflict and prevail throughout the story. In "A Cask of Amontillado," the advantage is always with Montresor; we know that poor Fortunato never has a chance. Critical moments occur during the development of the narrative when Fortunato could perhaps have escaped from Montresor's control had conditions been a little different. In these moments of crisis the conflict is varied, but there is no shift of advantage. Such crises are like turning points without turns; the advantage of one side may actually be increased.

Up to now we have been concerned with the pattern created by the working-out of the conflict. Related to, but not identical to that pattern, is the emotional or psychological pattern inherent in the plot, which we discuss in terms of climaxes. A climax is a point in a narrative in which the conflict comes to a head, is strikingly intensified for a time. The "big scene" in a play like *Hamlet,* which ends with the violent deaths of almost all the principal characters, is a climax, indeed the major one. But there are often other minor ones, the subclimaxes, before or after the major one. With the concept of a major climax in mind we use the terms "rising action" for the build-up to that climax and "falling action" for what follows it. This concept of the action's building up, perhaps through a series of striking events, to a central climax and then letting down again may or may not correspond closely to the pattern of the conflict.

Often the major climax and the turning point are the same event; sometimes, as in *Macbeth,* they are not. Sometimes the climax and the resolution are the same event, and sometimes not; they coincide in *Macbeth,* but not in Hemingway's "The Killers." In that story, a pair of gangsters appears at a diner in a small town and prepares to kill a certain Ole Anderson when he arrives; Anderson never comes, and when the gangsters finally leave, the young man, Nick, who had been tied up during the affair, runs off to warn Anderson. But Anderson knows that it is futile to try to escape, and Nick returns to the diner in bewilderment and horror, realizing that there is nothing he can do. All the exciting points in the story —the climaxes—come relatively early; when, at the end, Nick achieves the realization that constitutes the resolution of the conflict the event is understated. The falling action following the major climax (in the psychological pattern) is often different from the denouement following the resolution of the conflict.

Both the plot and the psychological pattern should be considered, for each embodies a certain kind of insight into narrative. We appreciate some stories—Poe's "Masque of the Red Death," which deliberately and primarily works on our emotions for its effect—by regarding their psychological pattern, while we profit more by stressing the pattern of the conflict in such narratives as *Macbeth.* And the two patterns coincide well enough, as indeed they must if a narrative is to be satisfactorily unified in its effect, to make it possible for us to consider them at the same time.

In order to summarize and clarify the two kinds of pattern, let us refer to the two diagrams of hypothetical stories:

A PSYCHOLOGICAL PATTERN:

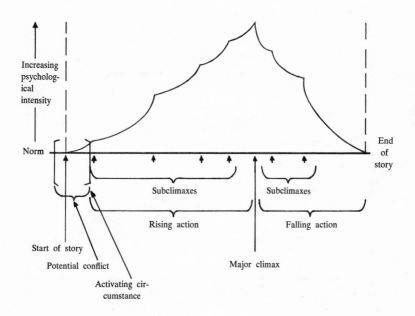

The first diagram shows the course of the story from the side, rising from the level of the normal hubbub of everyday life to a height of psychological intensity and then subsiding more rapidly. This is a common and representative pattern, though not the only one nor even the "normal" one. We must also be careful not to consider the heights of the climaxes as critical dimensions.

37

A PATTERN OF CONFLICT:

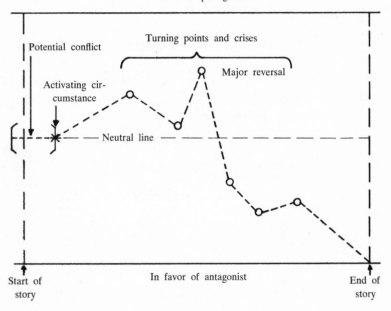

The second diagram represents the plot as if it were seen from above; it is intended to show the direction that the conflict takes, toward one side or the other, not rising and falling. This diagram, too, represents one possible pattern rather than a "normal" or typical one. The number of minor turning points and crises varies greatly, as do the proportions of the sections of the story.

38

The handling of plot and of the psychological pattern points up one of the principal characteristics of imaginative narrative, its structure. Such narrative is always a selection and ordering of experience, and we must recognize this explicitly in order to treat the work as literature—an art—rather than unformed life.

THE HANDLING OF TIME

The treatment of time-sequence also reveals the basic artistic nature of imaginative narrative, for writers commonly order experience—make it artistically coherent—by disarranging chronology. The events in a story are often presented in a different order and proportion from that in which they supposedly occurred.

Writers disarrange time in two main ways. The first way is to reorder it by presenting events out of their chronological sequence. The traditional literary epic, for example, begins *in medias res,* in the middle of things, and then later, by a retrospective narrative, reveals what has happened previously. Many other narratives begin in the midst of the action and then revert to the past by means of a summary of the events leading to the action or by a flashback which shows the events happening. These stories open in the middle of the development of the conflict and reveal the activating circumstance retrospectively. Other narratives skip back and forth several times between the present and the past; the practical limit to such variation is the necessity for continuity. Still, many stories achieve coherence by means of the time sequence and therefore do not modify chronology at all.

The second principal way of varying chronology is by expanding or contracting time. As E. M. Forster says in *Aspects of the Novel*[1], we all know that some of our experiences have been much more valuable than others that have occupied more time. Writers operate like our memories and present some events directly, in vivid

[1] New York, 1927, p. 49.

detail, and at great length, while summarizing or completely ignoring other, longer, episodes.

It is almost impossible to imagine reading a story in which we
see the hero getting up in the morning, brushing his teeth, getting
dressed, and eating breakfast at the same length and in as much
detail as we later see him, say, rescue the drowning heroine. If in a
story the trivia of existence were allotted the attention proportion-
ate to the time they took, the story would seem very badly propor-
tioned. Though writers could easily imagine what the hero might
be doing in his off hours, they will not waste their time or ours
doing so, for those trivia are not really part of the story. Writers
will ignore whatever irrelevant and unimportant action they might
imagine, summarize minor events, and reserve their powers of direct and vivid presentation for the episodes that are important to
them and to their stories. In those episodes they may cite every
work and gesture in order to let us see clearly and immediately
the crucial actions; they may even reproduce a character's thoughts
verbatim by the "stream-of-consciousness" technique.

Ernest Hemingway's "Short Happy Life of Francis Macomber"
is a good example of how time is modified for effect. First, the actual chronology of the material covered by the story is different
from the order in which it is presented. When the story opens, Macomber, his wife, and their guide, Wilson, are having a rather unpleasant lunch after the morning's hunting. That hunt, of a lion, is
next presented in a flashback through Macomber's recollections
that night; he had revealed in the hunt that he was a coward by
running away from the wounded lion's charge while Wilson stood
fast and shot the animal. The reader's impression of the lion hunt
is established by having witnessed the effect of Macomber's behavior on Mrs. Macomber, Wilson, and on Macomber himself. In
other circumstances running from a charging lion would be very
sensible, but the contempt that all the characters displayed at
lunch predisposes us against it. And the contempt also predeter-

mines our impressions of the buffalo hunt the following afternoon, in which Macomber acquires courage in the excitement of the chase.

Second, the important episodes in "The Short Happy Life" are presented at length and in detail. The lion and buffalo hunts are presented directly and vividly (much more so than the impala hunt in the morning of the second day, for instance), and the lunch-time conversation is reported in detail. Our impressions of the main characters and their interrelationships are determined precisely and clearly by this immediate evidence, and the significance of the lion and the buffalo hunts is precisely indicated. The ordering and proportioning of time, in this story as in others, signalize the essential nature and quality of the story. The particular character of a story depends more on the order and the relative extension of the events as presented than it does on their strictly chronological and causal sequence.

COHERENCE

A dual sequence of chronology and causation always exists in a plotted narrative, and certain common and important concepts reflect the necessity of maintaining the temporal and causal relation between events. The problem for the writer is twofold: he must prepare for events to come, and he must justify those that have happened.

The first and most necessary kind of preparation for the future is the "exposition," the process of providing information about the locale, the characters, and the situation at the beginning of the plot so that the story can be understood. This exposition may be as brief as the single line in "A Cask of Amontillado" ("The thousand injuries of Fortunato I had borne as best I could; but when he ventured upon insult, I vowed revenge") or it may be several pages long; it may be offered explicitly by the author speaking omnisciently and generally, as Dickens does in the opening pages of *A*

Tale of Two Cities ("It was the best of times, it was the worst of times . . . ."), or it may be indicated implicitly through the objective description of the scene and of the words and actions of characters, as in "The Killers." And it may be provided all at once at the very beginning of the story, or some of it may be delayed until the plot is well under way. *Oedipus* is an interesting case: the contrast between the brief background information given at the start of the play and that which emerges later illustrates how the exposition and the way it is handled can be crucial in a literary work. At the beginning we learn only that Oedipus' city-state is beset by a plague and that his brother-in-law Creon has been sent to the oracle to find out the reason; when Creon returns in the first scene, we learn from him that the murderer of the former king, Laius, is still in the city. During the course of the play, however—and indeed this is the main point of the plot—the whole terrible truth about Oedipus' past gradually comes to light in an extreme example of delayed exposition. The kind of question we must ask is, "What effect does the nature and location of the exposition have on the story?" It must at least give us enough information to prepare us for later events, or if it comes after the events, to justify them.

The exposition can justify an event either before or after it happens, but few stories depend heavily on surprizes that have to be justified afterward. The commonest technique for achieving coherence in narrative is to prepare for events beforehand both psychologically and logically, thereby developing suspense and making events probable when they occur.

Psychological preparation is suggesting that something is going to happen. Our natural tendency as readers is to want to know what happens next; we ask, "Now that this event has occurred, what will be the result?" We are intrigued by the various possible consequences of particular events and of the dominant general conflict. We feel that something is bound to happen, so that when it does, our expectations are fulfilled.

The consequences of events are also prepared for logically, so that when events occur we know the reason for them. They become probable because they are the kind of thing that reasonably happens, given the preceding events and the motivations of the characters. Without this logical preparation many events would seem too surprising even to be adequately justified afterward, and a story containing too many contrived and artificial events is rarely satisfying. Love at first sight, for example, has fewer legs to stand on than the love that finally unites Elizabeth and Darcy at the very end of Jane Austen's novel *Pride and Prejudice;* they start out by disliking each other, and it is only when they come to know each other very thoroughly that they fall in love—the event logically follows from the growth of their mutual understanding.

The logical preparation for developments in a story is usually taken care of by the chain of causation and motivation in the plot. Psychological preparation, however, often involves special techniques. In fact, one particular technique, "foreshadowing," is very common. We are all too familiar with such trite phrases as "Little did he know what dire events were to occur. . . ." These are obvious attempts to let the reader know that something is going to happen, to foreshadow the event. Fortunately, most foreshadowings are more graceful and more subtle. They are embodied in a character's gesture or a slip of his tongue, or in a casual remark or minor incident. If foreshadowings are obvious, they are so to good purpose. The meaning of the many remarks that Oedipus makes early in Sophocles' play about what will happen to King Laius' murderer when he is discovered is very clear to us, for we know before the play begins that Oedipus himself is, unknowingly, the murderer..For that reason, the ironic effect of the remarks is one of the notable features of the play. On the other hand, some foreshadowings are hardly perceptible until after the event, when we can look back and realize what a certain conversation or bit of action had suggested, though we did not perceive it at the time. For example, in Act II of Shakespeare's play, Lady Macbeth, having smeared Duncan's groom with blood after the murder, re-enters and hears Macbeth assert that his bloody hand, rather than be washed clean by the sea, will "the multitudinous seas incarnadine"; she then says "My hands are of your color but . . . / A little water clears us of this deed." When we reach the sleepwalking scene in Act V, an echo of the earlier scene is evoked with telling effect: we have been prepared psychologically for the later scene without realizing it. Foreshadowing is a deliberate artistic device which, well used, can sharply reinforce a narrative's coherence.

MORE ON POINT OF VIEW

To conclude our exploration of some of the subtleties and refinements of narrative, we should briefly reconsider the point of view. We may raise the question, first of all, whether the point of view in a given narrative remains the same from beginning to end. Usually, it does. Plays, as we have noted, are almost always entirely objective, at least as they normally appear on the stage, where the somewhat personal and omniscient stage directions are not available to the audience. And in nondramatic narrative, it seems logical that once the hero, say, begins to tell his story, he should be the one to finish it. Moreover, for the sake of unity of effect, if not logic, the point of view usually remains the same.

Sometimes it does change, however, obviously or subtly. Obvious changes are relatively rare, but there have been cases in which a work is told in the third person for the most part, but concludes with a chapter in the first person; there have also been detective novels in which each chapter is narrated by a different character (in such cases, the point of view remains generally "first person," but what is more important is that it changes from that, say, of the protagonist to that of a different major character to that of a minor character, and so on). We may wonder what effect such shifts have on the unity, but we will need to consider further what compensating virtues might result from a variety of points of view that would offset the apparent loss of coherence. Salinger's short story, "To

Esmé—with Love and Squalor," is a good case in point. The first half is narrated by the protagonist, while the second is presented by an omniscient author who refers to the protagonist in the third person. The protagonist was so disturbed by the war experiences that took place between the halves that in the latter part of the story he is almost literally "not himself." The shift in point of view brings out his psychological dislocation most dramatically.

Minor and more subtle shifts in point of view occur in almost all nondramatic narrative. Now and then writers will provide, in a basically objective story, certain information about background or about the contents of characters' minds which a camera or microphone could not pick up, and conversely they will often tell parts of a story relatively objectively when their basic point of view is omniscient. In "The Killers," for instance, when the killers leave the diner and the owner unties Nick and the colored cook, we are told that Nick had never had a towel in his mouth before, a piece of information that comes from an omniscient author rather than a completely objective record of the immediate events as in the rest of the story. In "The Short Happy Life of Francis Macomber," conversely, long passages are presented objectively even though we are usually allowed to know what Wilson and Macomber, at least, are thinking. The question, as always, is what is the effect on the story. In addition, we might note another kind of subtle modification of the point of view that occurs in this last story. During most of the narrative we follow Wilson's thoughts and feelings, seeing everything from his standpoint, although he is neither the narrator nor the protagonist; but in the flashback about the lion hunt, we are attached to Macomber, and even at one point to the lion (we are told how he feels when the bullet hits him). This kind of shifting is legitimate with the omniscient point of view, from which all knowledge is available, but it raises problems of identification. We usually assume that the reader will identify himself more or less with the character who serves as the focal point of the story, be he the narrator or, in most third-person narratives, the protagonist. What is the effect, then, in "The Short Happy Life" of making Wilson the primary focal point, and yet at times shifting the focus to Macomber, not to mention the lion? Certainly we tend to feel the way Wilson does most of the time, that is, we identify ourselves with him; but when the lion's sufferings are described, we cannot help feeling with him for the moment. These variations may produce a kind of objectivity, even a universal empathy, or they may direct our sympathies toward one person or another as the occasion and the ultimate point of the story demand, for we do have to understand the different attitudes of Wilson, Macomber, and even the lion in order to appreciate fully what happens to Macomber.

Finally, we should consider briefly the artistic principle underlying the point of view, the selection of the protagonist, and the question of identification: esthetic or psychical distance. This basic separation of the reader from the events of a story is inherent in the fact that art and life are separate and different. They are different partly because art reorders experience, and also because an artistic version of an experience does not have the immediacy that that experience would have in real life. We know that Othello does not really kill Desdemona on the stage so we do not run up and try to save her. Even if a reader identifies herself so closely with the heroine in a story that she weeps when the heroine suffers, she will read on with pleasure, for the experience is not actual but vicarious.

There are many ramifications of the problem of esthetic distance that we might explore. One of these is the question of the effect of different esthetic distances. If the reader identifies himself very closely with the protagonist or narrator of a story and participates intensely in vividly presented events, will his experience be better or worse than, or merely different from, his experience with a story whose characters and events are presented so objectively and perhaps are so abstractly symbolical that they inspire not sympathy but an intellectual dispassion? How close to real life can a literary work take us and still remain art, and how far into the abstract can it take us without becoming simply an intellectual exercise? More immediately, what is the effect in Conrad's *Heart of Darkness,* say, of having the story told by a narrator who is repeating in detail the story that another character tells him; and what effect on the esthetic distance is produced by the conjunction in "The Killers" of an almost completely objective point of view and a focus on a very sympathetic and likeable protagonist? Such considerations take us deeply into the nature of imaginative literature and therefore of art, and help show why we need to consider carefully the elements of literature and their subtleties and refinements.

Imagery and Figurative Language

BASIC TERMS AND CONCEPTS

Some elements of literature—those concerning the material, the structure, and the organization of imaginative literature—are relatively abstract concepts and can be applied to many different forms of art, even nonverbal ones, for a plot can be conveyed in pantomime, and characters and settings can exist in paintings as well as in literature. The techniques and concepts that concern us now are intrinsically literary, and they bring us down to the very stuff of literature, language.

IMAGERY

The first basic concept to consider, imagery, is applied mainly to poetry, though it has equal significance in prose fiction and drama. Anywhere an imaginative writer wishes by means of words to convey to his readers the physical quality of a thing or action, imagery is important.

Imagery is the "sensory content of a literary work."[1] It is the sense-impressions represented by the concrete words and phrases in the work. A concrete word is an image-making word, one which recalls to us a physical sensation or a number of them, as the word *table* recreates in our minds a visual impression of the piece of furniture that the word stands for. The collection of letters itself, the typography and the location on the page, produce a physical sensation which occasionally seems to match the word's referent (*blob* seems to some people to look like a blob), but that sensation is not what we are calling imagery. What is important here is not the word itself, but its referent, the thing or event that the word refers to.

The immediate function of imagery. The experience of imagery is an illusion. That is, the word *table* does not create a table for us, but merely reminds us of what a table looks like. We do not have the hallucination of seeing a table floating in the air before our eyes—at least normal people do not—but see it with our mind's eye. That experience is real enough and vivid enough to allow us to participate actively in the physical experiences described in a literary work. Thus, we can imagine the "damp ground," the "white web-work" of nitre on the walls of the catacombs of the Montresors, and the jingling of the bells on Fortunato's cap.

Instead of knowing abstractly that the narrator stopped on a snowy evening by someone's woods, in Frost's poem, we create in our minds a picture of the scene and perceive more clearly what the experience was for the narrator. It is worth noting that in the manuscript of the poem we can see how Frost worked toward clearer and more immediate imagery. One line, for example, was first written "Between a forest and a lake"; Frost changed the line to "Between the woods and frozen lake," making the imagery more

[1] Sylvan Barnet, M. Berman, W. Burto, *The Study of Literature,* Boston, 1960, p. 307.

vivid: the picture of a woods is more specific and limited than that of a forest, and "frozen lake" gives our imagination more to work with in recreating the sight than "lake" alone.[2]

The perception of imagery. If we are to "share" Frost's experience we must perceive the imagery. Most of us will perceive roughly the same imagery in a given work provided we pay attention to the words and phrases we read. It sometimes happens that various images are so closely linked in readers' minds with certain experiences that those readers can only with difficulty refrain from a personal response. If, for example, the images of snow and a dark winter evening in "Stopping by Woods" suggest to a particular reader a picture derived from his own personal experience of a howling blizzard, bitter cold, and frozen toes, that reader's interpretation of the poem would be faulty. He should see whether his interpretation is consistent with the rest of the poem, particularly with such lines as "The only other sound's the sweep / Of easy wind and downy flake," and correct his too-personal response. And at the same time, we must beware of the "stock response," which leads into too conventional an impression of the imagery in the context of particular works: in most people's minds the moon is associated with beauty and romance, but those impressions would be inappropriate in some ballads and ghost stories where it is an ill-omen.

Types of imagery. Since we need to become familiar with all the kinds of images, a somewhat more detailed analysis of imagery is necessary. Most people can form visual images fairly clearly, and as a result many people think that imagery is exclusively visual. This is not the case: the image in "the sweep of easy wind" is primarily auditory. So are some of the drunken porter's references to the knocking on the gate in Act II of *Macbeth;* so are the "whisper" from the telescreen in Winston's room and the description of the "hideous, grinding screech" at the Two Minutes Hate in *1984.*

[2] See Charles W. Cooper and John Holmes, *Preface to Poetry,* New York, 1946.

This last example is so specific a reference to a sound in the word *screech* that it is onomatopoeic—it both refers to the sound and actually imitates it.

There are as many kinds of images as we have general senses. Thus we distinguish the following: the visual, the auditory, the olfactory (smell), the gustatory (taste), and the kinesthetic (internal sensations). The sense of touch includes sensations of pressure, of heat, and of cold; the visual sense includes sensations of light and dark and of color. Sometimes these varieties of sensations are worth distinguishing in analyzing the imagery of literary works, but for practical purposes we usually limit ourselves to the six senses mentioned.

Visual and auditory images are quite common in imaginative literature. Tactile images, though not so common, are found in the "damp ground" of the Montresors' catacombs mentioned above, or the description of the old fisherman's rope-burned hands in Hemingway's *The Old Man and the Sea*. Keats offers examples of the relatively rare gustatory and olfactory imagery in the "candied apple, quince, and plum," and in "lavender'd" and "Filling the chilly room with perfume light" in stanzas XXX and XXXI of "The Eve of St. Agnes":

> And still she slept an azure-lidded sleep,
> In blanched linen, smooth, and lavender'd
> While he from forth the closet brought a heap
> Of candied apple, quince, and plum, and gourd;
> With jellies soother than the creamy curd,
> And lucent syrops, tinct with cinnamon;
> Manna and dates, in argosy transferr'd
> From Fez; and spiced dainties, every one,
> From Silken Samarcand to cedar'd Lebanon.
>
> These delicates he heap'd with glowing hand
> On golden dishes and in baskets bright
> Of wreathed silver: sumptuous they stand
> In the retired quiet of the night,
> Filling the chilly room with perfume light . . . .

The concept of kinesthetic imagery includes several kinds of sensations that have in common the fact that they are internal: the sense of balance, the sense of weight or of strain felt in the joints and muscles, the sensation of heaviness or nausea in the stomach. This type of imagery is uncommon, yet it is distinct from the other types, and can be very vivid indeed. Consider, for example, the "cramped hand that was almost as stiff as rigor mortis" that Hemingway's old man suffers with in his long battle with the great fish, or the phrase "zero at the bone" in Emily Dickinson's "Snake."

Finally, there is a way of presenting imagery called "synesthesia" that is a fusing of different sense-impressions, or the presenting of one kind of image in terms of a different kind. When Keats describes pain as "scarlet," or says in the "Ode to a Nightingale" that he "cannot see . . . what soft incense hangs upon the boughs" and mentions the light being blown by breezes, he makes use of synesthesia. We normally smell, rather than see, incense, and we see light instead of feeling it in a breeze.

As critical readers, we need to be reasonably conscious of these varieties of imagery at all times. This does not mean that we must be "tremblingly alive all o'er," as Pope put it in "An Essay on Man," but that we must register the appeals to our normal senses made in any literary work. Especially, we must register the effect of the imagery in correlation with the rest of the work it appears in. It is an important element of literature; some "Imagists" have even written poetry intended to manifest their belief that poetry's main purpose should be simply to make people perceive clearly and vividly the world around them, and we all agree that that perception is an important and satisfying variety of human experience. Furthering that experience is certainly one main function of literature, which imagery helps accomplish through very striking effects. It clarifies and makes precise the nature and quality of the experiences depicted, as we have seen in "Stopping by Woods." At the same time, it increases the immediacy and therefore the vividness of those experiences.

The ultimate function of imagery. The imagery embodies whatever meaning a work contains. It is much more than mere decoration, that is, interesting pictures and sensations put in to make ideas more lively. Even if an explicit statement of theme appears in a work, what it can encompass abstractly can never equal in richness and subtlety the total significance we perceive in the persons, places, and things.

Indeed, unless we see and hear and feel the subject matter, we are not reading imaginative literature, for the basic nature of such literature is to present to us physical as well as emotional experiences, and the intellectual experience is inherent in the physical and emotional ones.

Simile - like or as

FIGURATIVE LANGUAGE (METAPHOR)

Even more important than imagery in making us participate in a literary work is figurative language. The general term that we will use for the figures of speech that make up figurative language is *metaphor,* much as the term *imagery,* which narrowly refers to visual phenomena, is nevertheless used to cover other sense-impressions as well. Although figures of speech have been categorized extensively, with such terms as *simile, metonymy,* and *personification,* according to their structure or technique, we will concentrate here on the basic metaphorical process involved in all these *calling one thing by another name -* categories.

The basic process of metaphor is the <u>comparison of things that are largely dissimilar, but have at least some one characteristic in common.</u> Thus when the hump of the white whale, Moby-Dick, emerging from the sea is likened to a snow-hill, the comparison is based on the whiteness and smoothness of the snow-hill, not on its coldness, its chemical properties, or its location. When Frost in "Stopping by Woods" calls the flakes of snow "downy," he is not suggesting that they are made of organic material, but that they are soft, light, and fluffy. The comparison basic to metaphor, because

the pen is mightier than the sword -

don't mean pen + sword, mean written word and military battle it is selective, is nonliteral: the similarity between a snowflake and down is not close enough for them to be identical. When comparisons are made between nearly identical things, such as a book and a pamphlet, the process ceases to be figurative.

The metaphoric process. The steps we take consciously or unconsciously when we encounter a figure of speech are as follows. First, we realize that something is being compared, explicitly or implicitly, to something else: when Hamlet speaks of "a sea of troubles," he compares the sea with the collection of difficulties and problems he is facing. Next we realize that Shakespeare does not mean that Hamlet's troubles are literally an ocean; that is, we realize that the likeness is not perfect or complete. And finally, unless we are too literal-minded, we perceive the basis for the comparison, seeing the similarity and ignoring the dissimilarity; we see that although Hamlet's troubles are not wet and salty, they are multitudinous and almost overwhelming.

We usually take these steps so rapidly and unconsciously that the process seems simple. If the things compared metaphorically are not too dissimilar, if the likeness between them is relatively obvious, as it is in Frost's "downy flake" we have little trouble. But the less obvious the similarity, the more deliberate our analysis of the comparison is likely to be. To take the third step toward the significance of the figure of speech can be very difficult indeed. Consider the far-fetched (though not therefore bad) comparison at the beginning of T. S. Eliot's "Love Song of J. Alfred Prufrock": "the evening is spread out against the sky / Like a patient etherized upon a table." That Eliot is comparing one thing to another is easy to see from the word "like." That the two things are not literally alike is also, and shockingly, obvious. In fact, it is so obvious that they are dissimilar that we may wonder if we can possibly take the last step. Some literal-minded readers, indeed, cannot: they can see only that an evening and an etherized patient are almost totally unlike. We must consider rationally yet imaginatively what the basis for the comparison might be. What is the basis? It is a similarity of mood: like the patient, the evening is almost lifeless —sickly, deadened, vitiated.

A sophisticated reader easily perceives such intangibles, and indeed finds it rewarding to think of one thing in terms of something else that is superficially different. Saying abstractly that Hamlet's troubles are many and serious is not as satisfactory as comparing them to the sea. The associations and connotations that "sea" carries with it help suggest forcefully how Hamlet feels about his troubles. When we think of them as a sea we can feel the effect of those connotations even if we cannot identify them precisely.

Effective perception of metaphor. In order to get the best out of metaphor we should visualize its images just as clearly as necessary in order to perceive precisely the significance of the metaphor as presented. This means that we should note carefully the indicated connection between the elements compared. If the connection is vague and broad we must take the comparison generally, while if the connection is worked out in specific detail we must follow the analogy precisely so that its complex significance will emerge.

The need to take a general comparison generally can be seen in the case of the "sea of troubles." If we try to draw a close physical parallel between the two terms we are likely to find ourselves wondering whether Hamlet's troubles with the old busybody Polonius correspond to a wave or a whitecap. Trying to picture the metaphor too clearly betrays a kind of literal-mindedness: if Shakespeare says Hamlet's troubles are a sea, then we'll make them a sea even if we have to strain the metaphor to do it. In doing so, we lose sight of the point of the metaphor, which is the general similarity between the sea and the Prince's multitudinous and nearly overwhelming troubles.

The case is different when John Donne (an English poet of the seventeenth century) compares his and his wife's souls to the legs of a draughtsman's compass in "A Valediction: Forbidding Mourning":

If they be two, they are two so
    As stiff twin compasses are two;
Thy soul, the fixed foot, makes no show
    To move, but doth if the other do.

And though it in the center sit,
    Yet, when the other far doth roam,
It leans, and hearkens after it,
    And grows erect as that comes home.

Such wilt thou be to me, who must
    Like the other foot obliquely run:
Thy firmness makes my circle just,
    And makes me end where I begun.

The connection here is detailed and point-by-point; to comprehend the metaphor we must trace the analogy precisely. As always the main intent should be to perceive the intangible attitudes and ideas that the physical elements of the metaphor suggest. We should picture the images just clearly enough for the intangibles to emerge.

Particular virtues of metaphor. In "The Love Song of J. Alfred Prufrock," then, it does us little good to visualize very specifically "a patient etherized upon a table"; what we must stress is the mood of the evening which the comparison suggests. Many figures of speech are, like this one, based on intangibles rather than on qualities that would satisfy a "practical" reader. But it is only through the intangible qualities of metaphor that we can perceive exactly the atmosphere of Prufrock's evening. Metaphor is inherent not only in imaginative literature but in all speech and writing because of its precision, economy, and immediacy as well. Eliot's figure of speech conveys the mood of the evening more precisely than any abstract words or phrases could, and it is far more concise than any equally accurate direct description could possibly be. Figures of speech convey shades of meaning that cannot be expressed exactly any other way, they convey a great deal in a shorter time than would otherwise be possible, and they are immediate because they embody the meaning in imagery instead of expressing it abstractly.

SUBTLETIES AND REFINEMENTS

LITERATURE'S BASIS IN IMAGERY

We noted at the beginning of this chapter that the use of imagery is not peculiar to poetry, but occurs wherever a writer wishes to make the reader perceive the physical quality of an action or object. That imaginative literature does present that physical quality is evidenced by the concreteness of good poetry and by the emphasis on direct presentation in prose fiction and in drama. Writers vary in the amount, the kind, and the intensity of imagery, but almost all of them rely on it heavily.

That is to say, almost all imaginative literature is basically dramatic. To the extent that it actually shows the characters, the setting, and the action, and makes such intangibles as moods and feelings perceptible through our senses, a literary work is dramatic. A fundamental characteristic of drama is that it presents things directly for our eyes and ears to see and hear rather than merely telling us about them. All plays have this considerable virtue in common. It is particularly satisfying to see things for ourselves rather than merely hear about them, and drama provides that satisfaction.

Consider *Oedipus* once again. In one sense the play is uneventful: the action is almost all conversation, and its locale is always the same. When violence occurs, it happens off-stage, in accordance with Greek dramatic convention, and is simply reported. But we are not merely being told at second hand that Oedipus gradually found out about his sins and blinded himself. We are actually shown images of the king and Jocasta and the others, and can hear them speaking with each other before the palace at Thebes. Thanks to the director and the actors, we can see the ges-

tures the characters make, and hear the hoarseness or solemnity of
their voices. The basic function of drama is to let us see for ourselves. It is interesting to note how Sophocles' dramatic intentions
reveal themselves when he has to have a messenger report the violence that has taken place off stage within the palace. The information he has to convey is that Jocasta has killed herself and Oedipus has blinded himself, and the speech in which he reports this
is strikingly vivid and immediate in its imagery so that we can see,
vicariously, the violence and blood that make the events terrible.

The same process occurs in prose fiction: in the imagery we perceive the characters and events. The difference between a plot summary of a novel and a short story is not simply one of length, but
also of concrete detail. A plot summary tells us what happens,
while the short story actually presents the action for us to see and
hear. A narrative without imagery could have no direct dialogue, no
clear description of physical setting or actions, no specific information about the characters' physical appearance; in short, it would be
an abstract and lifeless impossibility. Thurber's "Secret Life of Walter Mitty" is worth examining in this connection: we are not simply
told what Walter Mitty daydreams about, but have those dreams
presented in full and complete detail, as if they were taking place
before our eyes—we even hear the "pocketa-pocketa" of "Com-
mander Mitty's" giant seaplane as it flies through the storm. We
can see for ourselves what Mitty is like from the immediate evidence of the imagery that makes the tenuous and intangible daydreams clear and vivid. We learn much more about Mitty than we
might if we were simply told abstractly what he was like.

Because prose fiction relies on direct presentation to achieve its
effects, it can often be successfully made into a play or movie.
Such a dramatization involves recreating physically the imagery in
the prose narrative. In the drama the imagery is presented by
means of the actors and the stage sets, rather than by the words.

It is hard to overemphasize the importance of imagery in literature. All of us are familiar with the "dryness" of an abstract lec-

ture or essay and with the life that concrete illustrations can infuse into the most technical and abstruse subject. This vividness, a principal characteristic of good imaginative literature, is the result of its imagery. An almost countless variety of sensations can be perceived, and a single experience usually involves many different sensations. How many, for example, are involved in the enjoyment of eating an apple? To begin with, think of the pleasure from the size, the shape, the color, and the weight of it.

Our eyes can register not only shapes and sizes, but light and dark, and various colors. Our ears perceive degrees of loudness, tone or timbre, harmony and discordance, and so forth. Similarly, our sense of taste reacts to sourness, bitterness, saltiness, and sweetness. Remembering these varieties of perceptions, we note them in our reading in order to see the effect they have in a poem or in a scene in a novel. Sometimes a particular kind of sensation is presented as a key to the total quality of a scene or is one of the main elements in it. Recall how precisely Orwell defines the sound that opens the Two Minutes Hate in *1984* (a "hideous grinding screech"), and how Browning helps characterize the "last Duchess" by repeatedly mentioning her blushing.

The variety of sense-impressions also indicates how imagery can sometimes be very precise. Instead of simply mentioning a tree in the fall, a writer may specify, as Shakespeare does in Sonnet 73, many details of the tree, such as the number or color of the leaves, and the motion of the branches:

> That time of year thou mayst in me behold
> When yellow leaves, or none, or few, do hang
> Upon those boughs which shake against the cold,
> Bare ruined choirs, where late the sweet birds sang.
> In me thou see'st the twilight of such day
> As after sunset fadeth in the west,
> Which by and by black night doth take away,
> Death's second self, that seals up all in rest.
> In me thou see'st the glowing of such fire
> That on the ashes of his youth doth lie,

As the death-bed whereon it must expire,
Consumed with that which it was nourished by.
    This thou perceiv'st, which makes thy love more strong,
    To love that well which thou must leave ere long.

The result of this precision is that the reader can perceive the effect, the quality, of the image much more definitely. As we have noted, however, it is not always so important to visualize an image clearly as it is to perceive its effect, its salient characteristics. Writers often emphasize the character of an image by making quite specific their references to especially effective details or particular sense-impressions. Yet this kind of precision is not always necessary. Wordsworth, in his sonnet "Composed upon Westminster Bridge," is very specific in citing the details of the city which he sees, and thereby achieves an admirable vividness and concentration:

> Earth has not anything to show more fair:
> Dull would he be of soul who could pass by
> A sight so touching in its majesty:
> This city now doth, like a garment, wear
> The beauty of the morning; silent, bare,
> Ships, towers, domes, theatres, and temples lie
> Open unto the fields, and to the sky;
> All bright and glittering in the smokeless air.
> Never did sun more beautifully steep
> In his first splendor, valley, rock, or hill;
> Ne'er saw I, never felt, a calm so deep!
> The river glideth at his own sweet will:
> Dear God! the very houses seem asleep;
> And all that mighty heart is lying still!

His method in "London, 1802," however, is different, yet equally successful. There, the images are more general and abstract; they are not immediately visible details but physical things used to represent a general tone or quality:

Milton! thou shouldst be living at this hour:
England hath need of thee: she is a fen
Of stagnant waters: altar, sword, and pen,
Fireside, the heroic wealth of hall and bower,
Have forfeited their ancient English dower
Of inward happiness. We are selfish men:
Oh! raise us up, return to us again;
And give us manners, virtue, freedom, power.
Thy soul was like a Star, and dwelt apart:
Thou hadst a voice whose sound was like the sea,
Pure as the naked heavens, majestic, free;
So didst thou travel on life's common way
In cheerful godliness; and yet thy heart
The lowliest duties on herself did lay.

A good deal of the power of the sonnet depends on the style and the sound-pattern, to be sure, but insofar as the imagery is effective, it produces a general, intangible force and attitude rather than specifying perceptible scenes. In other words, the imagery in "London, 1802" operates on a different level, a more intellectual one, than that in poems whose imagery is clearer and more precise.

Realizing that the physical images are not so important for their own sakes as for what they suggest, for their effect on the whole poem, we will recognize first that imagery cannot be considered all by itself. It is one of the many elements in a literary work, and even in poems it is not always the most important one. And second, imagery cannot always be distinguished from metaphor, nor from symbolism. Much of the imagery in "London, 1802," for instance, has a symbolic value: "a fen [marsh] of stagnant waters" certainly symbolizes the moral laxness that Wordsworth saw in England at that time. In other words, the physical things and sensations purveyed by a literary work are most often important for what they remind us of or suggest to us. Because imagery may suggest, or, better, embody, so much of the basic meaning and character of a work, it is important for us to understand how it is used.

CATEGORIES OF METAPHOR

The categories of metaphor that will concern us here are those that indicate how metaphor operates. In the first part of this chapter, we noted that figures of speech have been categorized formally as simile, metonymy, and so forth. We need not consider those classifications at length, for we are primarily interested in the function of metaphor, in what metaphor does for a literary work and how it does it, rather than its form. We will consider various categories based on the psychological or artistic nature of figures of speech. In other words, we want to know how the beast behaves, not how many toes it has. Our categories consist of four or five pairs of "opposites," hypothetical opposing extremes or poles between which all actual metaphors will fall. At the same time, particular metaphors will usually fall into several categories without inconsistency.

Live and dead metaphor. First, let us clear the ground by distinguishing between live metaphors and dead ones. A dead metaphor is one that has lost its figurativeness. The "foot" of the hill, for example, no longer implies a comparison between the base of the hill and a human foot, and it is the same with the leg of a table and the eye of a needle; the statements are no longer metaphorical, but literal. A live metaphor, on the other hand, is not a literal statement, as we have already observed in discussing Hamlet's "sea of troubles." We are conscious of the dissimilarity between a sea and Hamlet's collection of difficulties, and have to make some effort to discern the similarity. The effort in this case is not very great, and the metaphor is that much closer to dying, simply because the expression is so often used. Many figures of speech, in becoming clichés, have almost died (for example, a dog's life, dead as a doornail); they carry a certain raciness with them, but little or no metaphorical quality.

The more obvious the similarity between the terms of the metaphor, the more likely the figure is to die. The "jacket" of a book is so obviously like a man's coat in relation to the book that it was easy for the word to come to mean, literally, that paper wrapper, as well as the other similar things it stands for. On the other hand, the figure of the evening as an etherized patient at the beginning of "Prufrock" will never become so trite as to lose its life. Some readers, in fact, feel that it is too strained, too far-fetched, and therefore ineffective. In reading, we ask ourselves whether a given metaphor is alive but too strained, or felicitous but half-way to death.

Far-fetched and obvious metaphor. The far-fetched figure of speech and the obvious are the second pair of opposites. We know that either extreme raises problems and has drawbacks. Nevertheless, each has its particular advantages. A relatively obvious figure can seem so natural and even inevitable that it will be peculiarly satisfying, like Frost's "easy wind and downy flake" in "Stopping by Woods," or Hamlet's "the native hue of resolution / Is sicklied o'er with the pale cast of thought." Far-fetched metaphor, by shocking us briefly and enforcing our attention because of its difficulty, can also effectively arouse and intrigue us.

Before moving on to the next pair of opposites, we might note the term *conceit,* which is commonly used for a far-fetched figure of speech, though it arose in England in Shakespeare's day when a thirty- or forty-year vogue of such figures began. Many of the conceits invented during the vogue were strained and merely decorative (for example, the lover as a ship tossed by the storm produced by his own sighs and floods of tears), while others—many of Donne's for example—were compelling and effective.

Donne's most famous conceit is the one quoted above in which he shows how he and his wife can be separate yet joined and interdependent by comparing his soul and his wife's to the legs of a draughtsman's compass (in "A Valediction: Forbidding Mourning"). Similarly Milton's Homeric simile (one modeled on Homer's long similes) comparing the fallen Satan to a whale occupies some ten lines of *Paradise Lost:*

> Thus Satan . . .
> Lay floating many a rood, in bulk as huge
> As . . .   that sea-beast
> *Leviathan,* which God of all his works
> Created hugest that swim th' ocean stream:
> Him haply slumb'ring on the *Norway* foam
> The pilot of some small night-founder'd skiff,
> Deeming some island, oft, as seamen tell,
> With fixed anchor in his scaly rind
> Moors by his side under the lee, while night
> Invests the sea, and wished morn delays.
>   (Bk. I, 11. 192–208)

These are examples of extended figures as compared to brief ones like Frost's "downy flake." This, then, is our next pair of opposites.

Extended and brief metaphor. Our main question is about the particular functions and effects of the extended and the brief metaphor. One function of the brief metaphor is to characterize something vividly without impeding the flow of the literary work. A brief figure affects the reader without diverting his attention from the main line of development to the figure itself, especially if the figure is relatively obvious rather than far-fetched. The metaphor may be a minor decorative touch, or it can serve as one detail among many which add up to produce a general and subtle flavor or tone that might not emerge from a single extended figure. The metaphors in Frost's "The only other sound's the sweep / Of easy wind and downy flake" achieve their effect so unobtrusively that we are hardly conscious of them. The same can be true even when the figures are more far-fetched than Frost's. Stephen Spender, in his "Express," conveys the sound of a locomotive's starting by "The first powerful plain manifesto" and "the black statement of pistons," brief metaphors which, though far-fetched, are nevertheless effective without being distracting.

What, then, is the function of the extended figure of speech? It is sometimes that of drawing attention to itself: we notice Donne's compass figure because it is developed at length, and as a result, we pay more attention to the point that it makes, the major one in the poem (since he and his wife are linked, she need not mourn when he leaves). The same is true of Milton's whale figure in *Paradise Lost:* Satan's great size is important in Milton's characterization of him.

There are other reasons for the length of these two figures, however. An extended figure serves to call our attention to a major point, and, at the same time, is a necessary development of a complex analogy and a means of working up relevant implications or of establishing a particular tone. The analogy in Donne's figure is so complex that it must be worked out explicitly in order to be clear and effective. Without that development, we could not see all the pointed and telling details of the analogy. Then, as Milton develops his analogy it becomes evident that he not only establishes Satan's size, but also imbues the analogy with certain connotations that contribute to the characterization of Satan. The story told in the figure, of the fishermen who mistake a whale for an island and perish when it sinks, implies aspects of Satan beyond his size.

Explicit and concealed metaphor. The next pair of opposites are explicit and concealed metaphors. An explicit figure is one in which both terms of the basic comparison appear. Donne's compass figure is explicit, for we realize that he is comparing certain unlike things. Shakespeare's "sea of troubles" is explicit. Blake's "Tiger! Tiger! burning bright" is less explicit because the basic comparison between the tiger and a fire is not directly stated but simply implied. The case is the same when Montresor in "A Cask of Amontillado" refers to "the white webwork which gleams from the cavern walls," using the similarity between the trickles of white chemical deposits and a spider web to suggest the relationship between Montresor and the hapless Fortunato. If a metaphor is thoroughly concealed, or is to be perceived only upon precise analysis while still remaining "live," it is called "submerged." In Shakespeare's phrase, "the native hue of resolution," the word "native" embodies a submerged metaphor. It suggests that a robust color is the "natural inhabitant" of a resolute man's complexion, but we are hardly conscious of the implied comparison.

The more extended a figure is the more likely it is to be explicit; it is difficult for a thoroughly developed figure to be anything else. A concealed metaphor, therefore, tends to be brief. This correlation indicates some of the effects of concealed or explicit metaphor. Like an extended metaphor, the explicit figure tends to bring itself to our attention in order to make a subtle or complex analogy clearer, while a submerged metaphor may slide into our minds without our realizing it. Each process, in certain circumstances, has its advantages.

Dominant and minor metaphors. There is also a correlation between the brief and the extended types and our last pair of opposites, the minor and the dominant figure. A brief figure like Keats' "leaden-eyed despairs" in the "Ode to a Nightingale" may fit into the poem well, yet be relatively isolated and incidental and therefore minor. An extended figure, on the other hand, is more important: consider the position of Donne's compass figure and its relation to the basic theme of the poem—it is the concluding figure, and the one which states the relationship between Donne and his wife most precisely and comprehensively.

Often a particular metaphor will constitute the backbone of a whole poem, as does the analogy between a man's house and the soul's body in Shakespeare's Sonnet 146. That poem is composed of single dominant figure which is both extended and explicit:

> Poor soul, the centre of my sinful earth,
> [Thrall to] these rebel powers that thee array,
> Why dost thou pine within and suffer dearth,

Painting thy outward walls so costly gay?
Why so large cost, having so short a lease,
Dost thou upon thy fading mansion spend?
Shall worms, inheritors of this excess,
Eat up thy charge? Is this thy body's end?
Then, soul, live thou upon thy servant's loss,
And let that pine to aggravate thy store;
Buy terms divine in selling hours of dross;
Within be fed, without be rich no more.
    So shalt thou feed on Death, that feeds on men,
    And Death once dead, there's no more dying then.

At the beginning of the poem, the poet asks why the soul spends so much on outward decoration, since it has "so short a lease" on the body; at the end, the soul is advised to take more care to itself and let its mansion go.

It is possible, nevertheless, for the dominant figure to consist not of a single extended metaphor, but of a series or group of brief figures whose interrelationship gives them the cumulative and pervasive importance of a single extended figure. Such a series is called a "motif." The metaphorical images of light and dark in the poem "Dover Beach," by Matthew Arnold, have such an importance. They suggest the general contrast that he found in his time between the light of religious faith that was failing before the encroaching darkness of doubt and uncertainty, but they are not emphatically or consecutively developed; instead, they are scattered through the poem, forming part of its general texture. By being closely interrelated, the figures constitute a single major figure of speech, but one that is exhibited not in one extended passage but in different aspects at various times.

IMAGERY, METAPHOR, AND SYMBOLISM

Identifying the dominant or important figures of speech in a work is complicated by the interrelationship already mentioned between imagery, metaphor, and symbolism. An image may be part of a figure of speech, to begin with—"leaden," in Keats' phrase "leaden-eyed despairs," is a case in point. Or an image may itself amount to a submerged metaphor, as do the words "feed" and "taste" in Keats' "Ode on Melancholy":

> . . . if thy mistress some rich anger shows,
> Emprison her soft hand, and let her rave,
> And feed deep, deep upon her peerless eyes . . .

> His soul shall taste the sadness of [Melancholy's] might,
> And be among her cloudy trophies hung.

At the same time, many images are symbolic: we can cite such obvious cases as William Blake's tiger, in the poem of that name; and in prose fiction, Nathaniel Hawthorne's *The Scarlet Letter*. Blake asks suggestively, "What immortal hand or eye / Could frame thy [the tiger's] fearful symmetry," for example, and Hawthorne's visible symbol of adultery is too well known to need comment.

The distinction as well as the connection between imagery, on the one hand, and metaphor and symbolism, on the other, must also be touched on in order to clarify our analysis. Briefly, an image is something perceived sensorily which does not directly suggest an analogy to something else. When such an analogy is suggested, an image will also be metaphorical or symbolic. Thus, in Browning's "My Last Duchess," the word "blush" in line 31 is a straightforward image. In "the faint / Half-flush that dies along her throat" (11. 18-19), the image, "dies," is also metaphorical because a flush "dies" only by analogy. And the bronze statue mentioned at the end of the poem—"Neptune . . . / Taming a sea-horse"—is more than imagery, for it suggests the relationship that the Duke desires with any Duchess of his.

Imagery, metaphor, and symbolism are vital to literature. Critics have argued in particular that metaphor, by making striking comparisons, provides us with new perceptions of the nature of things and the relations between them, and therefore suggests unifying patterns in our universe. Symbolism, in turn, is seen as the main way that man conceives of the abstract and general, in literature as in other fields. And the root of both symbolism and metaphor in literature is imagery, for symbols and metaphors are almost always images to begin with. Even when imagery is not figurative, however, it embodies an essential characteristic of literature, the sensory impressions that constitute our perceptions of the characters, objects, and actions that are the subject matter of literature.

symbolism - when
a metaphor is used
throughout a work

4 ✷✷✷✷✷✷✷✷✷✷

Sound Effects and Rhythm

BASIC TERMS AND CONCEPTS

In the first three chapters, we have dealt with techniques and concepts that apply to the subject matter of imaginative literature; that is, we have been analyzing the events and the people featured in literature, and the objects and phenomena embodied in the individual words that compose it. Now we shall consider some of the characteristics of the words themselves rather than what they refer to. The nature of a literary work is determined not only by what the words represent, but also by their sound. We need for two reasons to have a thorough understanding of these sounds—such as rime and rhythm—and of the effects they can produce. To begin with, these sounds and sound effects may constitute the rules of the game on many occasions. The prosodic form of a sonnet, to take a familiar example, is one of the dimensions of the poem that we must know just as we must know the basic rules of football or tennis in order to follow a game. The second and more important reason is the fact that the sound effects and the rhythm, in prose as well as in poetry, are methods of creating tone and meaning. The long, rolling sounds and rhythms of Milton's blank verse are highly significant to the general dignity and seriousness of *Paradise Lost,* just as the abrupt rhythms and the flat and simple sound effects of Hemingway's short stories help to establish the objectivity of their tone. And these examples represent only general effects; other more particular effects can be seen in specific instances. Indeed, we can see in many cases a clear analogy between the literary work and a piece of "program music" like Prokofiev's *Peter and the Wolf.* There, the events and characters are represented by the various "themes" and other musical elements, and are at the same time suggested by them: the theme that represents the cat sounds catlike, and the duck-theme sounds ducklike. Similarly, when the action represented is rapid, the tempo of the music speeds up correspondingly. The same kind of correspondence between the subject matter and the vehicle that conveys it can be seen in literature, as we can clearly recognize in the correlation between the smooth, low sound and rhythm of the first stanza of Gray's "Elegy Written in a Country Churchyard" and the scene it describes:

> The Curfew tolls the knell of parting day,
> The lowing herd wind slowly o'er the lea,
> The plowman homeward plods his weary way,
> And leaves the world to darkness and to me.

Before we examine such sounds and the patterns they may form, two words of warning are in order. First, we must rid ourselves of any assumption that all writers, particularly poets, sit down with an idea or subject they want to write about and deliberately figure out what sounds will best get that material across. A poet is unlikely to say to himself consciously, "I want to write about the serenity of the ocean, so I'll have to use a lot of *l*'s and *s*'s to convey that idea." This kind of process may occur, but usually a writer's creative thinking is more spontaneous than that. In the first place, most writers think of their subject matter and their technique as a complex unity, a synthesis. As critics, we can distinguish between them to some extent for the purpose of analysis, but for most writers, the two are organically united in the actual process of literary creation. Furthermore, writers think more in terms of expressing or embodying their material to their own satisfaction than of "getting it across" to their readers. Of course, most writers like to be read widely, but if that were all they liked, they would write nothing but pot-boilers.

The second word of warning is this: the sounds we will consider, and the patterns they form, have general and variable effects that depend on their context; they do not automatically produce a specific effect. An *m* can be the sound of a dove, but it can suggest other things, too; the sound is not even always soothing. A pentameter couplet often conveys a sense of finality or precision, especially in Pope, but various poets, including Pope, have modified this effect according to circumstances. These verbal devices do have suggestive power, and we can often appreciate their effect even if we are unable to define that effect precisely. But we must realize that the sounds appear in a context. Other elements of literature—the imagery and figures of speech, the sentence structure, indeed the subject matter—must always be taken into account when we analyze the nature and effect of the sound-pattern of a particular work.

Our two warnings, in other words, mean that we should remember that a literary work is fundamentally a compound, in the chemical sense, rather than a mixture whose ingredients are mechanically thrown together without affecting each other. At the same time it is a compound mixed by an experimenter who follows general, rather than precise, directions about what ingredients he should use, and how to mix them. To speak more literally, we should refrain from oversimplifying the sound-pattern, and from conceiving of it as a cut-and-dried set of devices.

First, we should make a distinction for clarity's sake between sound effects proper and rhythm. Rhythm in literature, as the word is usually used, depends on sound—on the repetition of it, that is. It is the repetition rather than the sound itself that is important, as witness the fact that rhythm can be produced by sights or other sensations: a row of telephone poles flashing by a car or train window produces rhythm soundlessly. Sound effects proper comprise, in literature, such things as rime (also spelled rhyme), alliteration, and assonance, all of which are derived directly from the sounds of the words themselves.

Rime. The most obvious and familiar sound effect is rime, which, loosely, is the similarity of the sounds at the ends of words. This definition must be framed loosely if it is to cover the different kinds of rime. Most conventionally, only "perfect" rimes are thought of by that name, but as any handbook on versification will reveal, there are also near-rimes, assonantal rimes, sight-rimes, and other varieties which have been used prominently enough to warrant definition. Our first step toward an understanding of rime should be to perceive the basis of the phenomenon and to recognize that there are different manifestations of that basis.

Rime is based on the similiarity of sounds, specifically those at the ends of words. We call a "perfect" rime one between words whose initial sounds are different, but whose last stressed vowel sound and all following consonant or vowel sounds are identical (sea-tea-lee, pain-rein-plane, and vacation-ovation, but not speak-bead-dead, or nature-future). Usually, we feel that the closer the identity of the sound, the better the rime is. Again, there is an exception: using completely identical words—that is, using exactly the same word for the sake of the rime (light-light)—is usually frowned on; the use of homonyms (see-sea) for rimes also seems a little questionable, for some reason.

Our usual preference for perfect rimes should not make us dismiss "near-rimes" and "sight-rimes." "Swan" can rime with "stone," "term" with "learn," "version" with "assertion," "miscreant" with "pant." These "near-rimes" are based on similarity, rather than identity, of sound. They range from cases like "term-learn" (in which almost all the requirements for a perfect rime are met), through "assonantal rimes" like "swan-stone" (in which the stressed vowel sound is similar but not identical), to rimes like "wrote-lit" (in which only the final consonant sounds are the same). "Sight-rimes" are those based on identical spelling, not on sound: "anemone-one." We must be tolerant of these near-rimes and sight-rimes, for we will find that they can be used very effectively. We should note, however, that perfect rimes are the most common, assonantal and other near-rimes somewhat less so, and sight-rimes relatively rare.

We can also set up a frequency scale on the basis of the number of syllables involved in the rime (one in "móon-sóon"; two in "féllōw-méllōw"; three in "dédicate-prédicate"), or on the basis of the number of unaccented syllables following the last stressed one (in féllōw-méllōw, there is one; in dédicate-prédicate, there are two). Such multiple rimes (involving more than one syllable) and "masculine" or "feminine" rimes (ending in a stressed syllable or in an unstressed syllable) can be important on occasion; they are, for example, two of the reasons for the bantering, impudent tone in Byron's *Don Juan:*

> In Seville was he born, a pleasant city,
> Famous for oranges and women—he
> Who has not seen it will be much to pity,
> So says the proverb—and I quite agree;
> Of all the Spanish towns is none more pretty,
> Cadiz perhaps—but that you soon may see:—
> Don Juan's parents lived beside the river,
> A noble stream, and called the Guadalquivir.

The most common and obvious function of rime, which we must recognize now, is its establishing of a relationship between lines of poetry.

By repeating at the end of a line the sound that ends a previous line, a poet suggests a connection between those lines. But a basic problem is implied in this definition: for a connection to be apparent the reappearance of the rime has to be fairly close—within five or six lines, say—or else the riming lines have to be connected in some other way in addition, by the position of the lines in a stanza, or by their subject matter. If the rime of the first line of a poem reappears at the end of the second, we see an obvious connection between the two; if the same rime reappears in lines 30 and 31, however, do we perceive a connection across the space of twenty-eight lines, or will we have forgotten the rime-sound and consider the rime in lines 30 and 31 new?

If rimes are relatively close they set up a connection between lines more or less independently of the subject matter and of other prosodic elements in a poem. The function of this connection is not always clear or unambiguous—in fact it may be multiple—but almost certainly the most common function of rime is structural. The pattern of rimes, called the rime scheme, acts as a kind of framework for the poem. The particular forms in which rime schemes may be set up and the nature of the structure they impose are many. It is best for us not to try to define every possibility, but rather to describe the various general kinds of rime schemes, identifying the extremes as far as possible.

To begin with, rimes may be distributed more or less regularly; that is, they may at one extreme occur in as regular a pattern as Alexander Pope's couplets,

> True wit is nature to advantage dress'd;
> What oft was thought, but ne'er so well express'd;
> Something, whose truth convinc'd at sight we find,
> That gives us back the image of our mind.

while at the other extreme they might conceivably be distributed almost at random. Admittedly a completely haphazard distribution would amount to no scheme at all, and would negate many of the valid functions of rime. The point to perceive here is that many poets have deliberately avoided simple, repetitive patterns of rime and instead have given their poems rime schemes that seem very irregular. Coleridge's "Kubla Khan," for instance, intermingles couplets, alternate and closed quatrains (abab and abba, respectively), and even triplets (aaa). Further toward the extreme is Frost's "After Apple-Picking," which has only a few recognizable quatrains and couplets: the scheme of the first five lines is abbacc, but that of the last ten is pgrpgststr.

Another way in which rime schemes may vary is in their continuity in a given poem. In other words, a poem at one extreme consists of a continuous series of rimed couplets, while at the other extreme a poem like Wordsworth's "Immortality" ode consists of stanzas of different lengths, each with a different rime scheme. Wordsworth's ode is practically a group of separate short poems on the same topic. Between these two extremes we would place such poems as Keats's odes. These poems are stanzaic, and the scheme within each stanza is moderately complicated—that of the "Ode on Melancholy," for instance, is ababcdecde—yet all the stanzas in a particular poem follow the same scheme (with a minor exception in the "Ode on a Grecian Urn"). The repetitiveness of the rime scheme makes for continuity, while the variations within it makes it less continuous than Pope's couplets. Also between the two extremes is Frost's "After Apple-Picking"; indeed, it could be argued that it has less continuity in the rime scheme than Wordsworth's ode, since its scheme is less repetitive—the "Immortality" ode does contain many quatrains and couplets, which, without occurring regularly, nevertheless constitute a kind of repetition that makes for continuity. The division of a poem into stanzas, however, especially stanzas of different lengths and rime schemes, does break up the continuity markedly. In other words, a poem's continuity depends on the arrangement of the lines as well as on the rime scheme proper, though that arrangement is usually correlated with the rime scheme.

A third type of variation in the pattern of rimes is in the complexity. Again, couplets will serve as an illustration of one extreme, that of simplicity, and alternate or closed quatrains are almost as simple. For an example of extreme complexity, we can cite Frost's poem again, except that its rimes seem to be distributed relatively haphazardly rather than organized according to a scheme. Their lack of regularity makes their pattern (such as it is) complex, of course, but even perfectly regular rime schemes may be complex. We have noted that moderate complexity of Keats's odes; still more complicated is the stanza Spenser devised for his "Epithalamion," which rimes ababccdedeefggffhh. This scheme is regular enough in the sense that it is composed of recognizable, conventional units like quatrains and couplets, and it is regular also in the fact that it is repeated in successive stanzas. Yet it is obviously complicated and even, therefore, ambiguous.

We call it ambiguous because the rime units within the stanza can be grouped in various ways—the last few lines, for example, can be grouped fgg ffh h, fggf fhh, eef ggff hh, or otherwise. This inherent ambiguity introduces structural problems that cannot be solved without considering what Spenser says in the stanza, how he organized it internally—that is, how he developed the subject matter. Let us defer considering that problem until later, taking it as a reminder now that the rime scheme must be considered in relation to the other elements of a poem.

At the opposite extreme from Spenser, such rime schemes as that of the Shakespearean sonnet are structured independently of the subject matter. The pattern is clear: ababcdcdefefgg falls into a group of twelve lines (or "douzaine" as it is sometimes called) composed of three quatrains, followed by a separate couplet. There is no inherent ambiguity here.

One reason for our certainty about the Shakespearean scheme is that the actual sounds of the rimes change at particular intervals; and this matter of the variety in sounds is another basis for a general distinction between rime schemes. To perceive this distinction we might contrast "After Apple-Picking" or one of Pope's poems in couplets with some of the French lyrical forms that have occasionally been used in English poetry. Frost's poem, in its forty-two lines, has eighteen different rime sounds; a poem in couplets of the same length would have twenty-one separate sounds. At the other extreme, a *ballade,* in its twenty-eight lines, has only three different rime sounds—its scheme is ababbcbc ababbcbc ababbcbc bcbc; and a *villanelle* has nineteen lines and but two rimes, for it is composed of five stanzas rimed aba and a sixth rimed abaa. These latter forms are very difficult to write in English, because of the relative scarcity of perfect rimes in the language, and are therefore rare. Two modern examples are Richard Wilbur's "Ballade for the Duke of Orleans," and Dylan Thomas' famous villanelle, "Do Not Go Gentle into That Good Night."

The next distinction is between the traditional or conventional rime schemes and the original ones. A traditional scheme is one that has been used by many poets for many years, while a conventional scheme has a set and recognized pattern. Since there is a connection between the two, however, we place both of them at one extreme, and complete originality at the other. Again there is a continuum between the extremes. The Shakespearean sonnet clearly has a conventional and traditional scheme, while "After Apple-Picking" is almost at the extreme of originality. A completely random distribution of rimes would be the only really original scheme, however; those poems like Frost's, or like "Kubla Khan," are partly conventional because the units—couplets, quatrains, triplets—that compose their rime schemes are in themselves conventional enough, even if their arrangement is not. At the same time, poets have modified the Shakespearean sonnet form, for example, in various ways (for instance, abab bcbc cdcd ee) that make it less purely conventional. One variation is especially interesting, that of Keats; from conventional and traditional elements (the alternate quatrain found in the Shakespearean sonnet, and a sestet of the Italian sonnet) he fashioned the original stanza for his odes: ababcdecde. Since conventions change, some traditional forms seem more conventional than others; "heroic quatrains" (abab cdcd, etc.) are more familiar to us now than is "rime royal" (stanzas rimed ababbcc) which was once very popular (see Shakespeare's long narrative poem, "The Rape of Lucrece"). Undoubtedly it is the simpler traditional forms like couplets and quatrains that now for various good reasons seem most conventional to us, rather than the complex forms like rime royal, the Spenserian stanza (ababbcbcc), and *ottava rima* (abababcc). The Shakespearean sonnet is worth citing as an exception, of course: it is complex, but quite familiar because it is still commonly used (and commonly taught in school). In other words, it is both traditional and conventional, for it has been used by many different poets for a long time, and it is familiar enough to us now to be easily recognizable.

This "recognizability" of the sonnet brings up yet another variable quality of rime schemes, that of their conspicuousness. Some schemes strike the ear clearly and immediately, while others are hardly noticeable until we look for them. This quality does not depend entirely on the schemes themselves, for there are readers sensitive enough to perceive even the subtlest sound-pattern, while untrained readers might not at first be conscious of even such an obvious rime scheme as that of Browning's "My Last Duchess" (couplets). Nevertheless, certain types of schemes and certain ways of handling them make them more or less conspicuous. Basically, the simpler, more repetitive, more regular, and more conventional the scheme is, the more conspicuous it is. Thus the alternate quatrains in A. E. Housman's "With Rue My Heart Is Laden" and the aaba bbcb scheme in "Stopping by Woods" are quite obvious:

> With rue my heart is laden
> For golden friends I had,
> For many a rose-lipt maiden,
> And many a lightfoot lad.

> (Housman)

Whose woods these are I think I know.
His house is in the village though;
He will not see me stopping here
To watch his woods fill up with snow.

(Frost)

"After Apple-Picking," on the other hand, may sound at first almost like blank verse.

My long two-pointed ladder's sticking through a tree
Toward heaven still,
And there's a barrel that I didn't fill
Beside it, and there may be two or three
Apples I didn't pick upon some bough.
But I am done with apple-picking now.
Essence of winter sleep is on the night,
The scent of apples: I am drowsing off.

And the shorter the lines, the more conspicuous the rimes, too. But why do some readers not notice the simple, regular, repetitive, and conventional couplets of "My Last Duchess"? The answer is that Browning did not, as Pope did, write the poem in end-stopped lines, but carried his clauses and phrases through the ends of the lines on into the middle of succeeding lines. Rarely did he bring the rimes to our attention by stopping us at the end of a line with a punctuation mark. The way Browning handled the rime in conjunction with the phrasing of the sentences in this case makes the scheme inconspicuous.

There is no real reason to feel that it is good or bad for a rime scheme to be conspicuous; no value judgement is implied here. Yet at one end of the scale, some readers ask "What's the use of rimes if no one notices them?" and at the other end, readers complain about rime schemes so obtrusive that they distract our attention from the subject matter. These problems become especially acute when we begin to consider seriously the relationship between the rime scheme and the organization of the subject matter of a poem; that is, between the external framework, as it were, and the internal organization. A final and important variable characteristic, then, of rime schemes is this: at one extreme, the rime scheme and the internal organization may be perfectly correlated, while at the other, they may be independent. An example of almost perfect correlation is Shakespeare's Sonnet 73, quoted on page 59. There the 4-4-4/-2 line division suggested by the rime scheme corresponds perfectly with the internal structure: each quatrain presents a separate but parallel figurative description of the poet's age, and the final couplet draws the total conclusion. Note, though, that the rime scheme of the Shakespearean sonnet (abab cdcd efef gg) is unambiguous: it clearly forms the particular pattern mentioned, and thus puts us in a position to see precisely whether the internal and external structures coincide. Many rime schemes are not so regular or definite, as we noted in connection with Spenser's "Epithalamion" stanza. For a modern example, consider Frost's "Fire and Ice," which rimes abaabcbcb. This sequence by itself might suggest several different patterns (for example, a/baab/cbcb, or aba/abc/bcb), and in fact seems rather irregular. It is only when we consider the rimes in relation to the internal structure that we can make a choice among the alternative patterns, finding that ab/aa/bcbcb reflects best the way the subject matter is developed.

> Some say the world will end in fire,
> Some say in ice.
> From what I've tasted of desire
> I hold with those who favor fire.
> But if it had to perish twice,
> I think I know enough of hate
> To say that for destruction ice
> Is also great
> And would suffice.

The moral of this example is two-fold: first—as we noted above —we cannot treat the rimes as if they appeared in a vacuum; second, rime schemes that seem irregular at first often are actually quite "regular" in a more fundamental sense by virtue of their relationship with the internal structure of the poems.

This kind of correlation between rime scheme and internal structure would seem to be the natural thing for a poet to aim at, yet the fact remains that many poets have not done so. In "My Last Duchess" the duke's monologue flows through or over the rimes, so that we almost ignore them as we read. Similarly, some of Milton's and Wordsworth's sonnets are developed internally with little regard for the structures suggested by the rimes, although in these cases we may notice the rime schemes, because the sonnet form is so familiar, and feel distracted by them. These last two are the kinds of cases in which the problems mentioned above become acute: the rime schemes seem too inconspicuous, if we don't notice them, obtrusive, if we do. Whether they really are ineffective remains to be seen after we consider other functions of rime besides the structural.

So far, we have been dealing with the schemes produced by end rimes, those that appear at the ends of verses (lines of poetry). We should also note that "internal" rime (rime involving words within a verse) is sometimes employed, and that it can help determine, or contribute to, the prosodic structure of a poem. The first line of Shakespeare's song "Hark, hark! the lark at heaven's gate sings" contains internal rime, as does occasionally Coleridge's "Ancient Mariner":

> The ice was here, the ice was there,
> The ice was all around:
> It crack'd and growl'd, and roar'd and howl'd,
> Like noises in a swound!

But these instances do not contribute significantly to the structure of the poems because they are occasional and intermittent. The structural use of internal rime is rare; one may find it, however, in the drinking song, "Back and Side, Go Bare, Go Bare," from the early English farce *Gammer Gurton's Needle* (c. 1553), in which the main stanzas regularly have the following pattern:

Though I go bare, take ye no care,
I nothing am a-cold;
I stuff my skin so full within
Of jolly good ale and old.

This kind of sound effect is fine, of course, for popular songs and humorous verse.

Like most other technical elements of literature, rime and rime schemes are based on settled but general principles which are subject to many variations. We have considered those principles and some of the major variations in order to provide ourselves with sufficient knowledge to approach poetry critically. We must be prepared to see further than the naive or unskilled reader, who pays little conscious attention to rime schemes unless they are especially conspicuous. What the naive reader overlooks is that the rime exerts its influence on him even when he is not conscious of it, just as a gradual cooling of the temperature on a hot summer day will make us feel more comfortable long before we begin to realize that the temperature is changing.

Sound effects other than rime. We have so far dealt only with rime. There are other elements in the sound pattern of a literary work, elements often less obvious than rime, but more widely significant because they are commonly found in both poetry and prose. These elements are alliteration, assonance, and onomatopoeia, not to mention less basic concepts like cacophony and euphony, which we need not concern ourselves with now. There is nothing abstruse or difficult about the basic concepts we are dealing with here. In fact onomatopoeia and alliteration, at least, are probably already familiar to most readers.

Onomatopoeia is easy to identify. It is the reproduction of the sound that a word stands for by means of the sound of the word itself, for example, crash, moan, thud. Edgar Allan Poe's poem "The Bells" comes to mind quickly as an illustration: " . . . the jingling and the tinkling of the [silver] bells," and the "clang, and crash, and roar" of the brazen bells—ll. 14 and 54. We can also think of passages in prose that will serve the same purpose. The voice of Cathy's ghost in *Wuthering Heights* "wails," Stubb "roars" at the sailors in *Moby-Dick,* and so forth. This reproduction of sound may seem a rather obvious technical trick when overemphasized, because it unites the sound effect with the suggestive power of auditory imagery. An onomatopoeic word not only names a sensation, as an image-making word does, but actually reproduces it, too.

In a slightly different category, because they are sound effects pure and simple, are alliteration and assonance. Alliteration is usually defined as the repetition of initial consonants: "this *p*etty *p*ace," "life's *f*itful *f*ever" (both from *Macbeth*). This definition needs to be modified, however, in order to be accurate and useful. In the phrase "life's fitful fever," to begin with, the initial *f*'s are not the only ones that count; an accurate conception of alliteration should also include the *f*'s within the words. The term "hidden alliteration" is sometimes used for these internal sounds; with less justification, "consonance" has been used the same way. For most critics and students, "alliteration" refers to both the initial sounds and the internal sounds, though primarily the former. Thus in Tennyson's famous line (from "Come Down, O Maid") "The moan of doves in immemorial elms," all the *m*'s are linked, as well as the two *l*'s, by alliteration, most of which is supposedly "hidden."

At this point you may remember Pope's phrase, "Apt alliteration's artful aid," in which the initial vowel sounds are intended to illustrate the technique named. When the repeated vowels are as conspicuous as these, their effect is very like the examples of alliteration cited above. But the term generally used for repeated vowel sounds, initial or internal, is "assonance":

"In X*a*n*a*d*u* did K*u*bl*a* Kh*a*n" (Coleridge),

"*I*, too, d*i*sl*i*ke *i*t . . ." (Marianne Moore, "Poetry").

We should recall a point made earlier in connection with near-rime, that the repeated sounds need not be absolutely identical. For example, it can be said that "*s*weet *sh*owers" ("shoures soote" in the original: Chaucer's *Canterbury Tales*) or "that one *t*alent which is *d*eath to hi*d*e" (Milton, "On His Blindness") both constitute alliteration, for the sounds are similar enough to establish an effective link. This dependence on similarity rather than identity of sound is common in assonance, especially; a strong link can be formed between slightly different vowel sounds if their pitch and their length are alike. In the line from Wordsworth, "I w*a*ndered l*o*nely as a cl*ou*d," assonance is established because the italicized vowel sounds are all long and relatively low, while the vowels in "mode" and "mad," or "clan" and "clean," on the other hand, are not close enough in length or pitch for effective assonance. Within certain limits, then, "near" alliteration and assonance are effective in a subdued and vague way, a way that can be distinctly advantageous in some circumstances.

Finally, we come to the use of certain consonants and vowels (even singly—that is, not alliterative or assonantal) in preference to others in particular circumstances. To illustrate: in Tennyson's line, " . . . the spires / Pricked with incredible pinnacles into heaven" (from "Holy Grail"), the short *i*-sounds as well as the various consonants have obviously been chosen in preference to long *o*-sounds, for example. The same phenomenon occurs in "The murmurous haunt of flies on summer eves" (Keats, "Ode to a Nightingale"), where the *m*'s, the *r*'s, and the *s*'s, as well as the vowels, are emphasized. This latter case is partly onomatopoeic, of course, not only in the word "murmurous," but also when similar sounds appear later. In the case of Tennyson's lines, the use of *i*'s is not onomatopoeic, but those sounds are nevertheless especially appropriate to the subject matter.

To illustrate the extent and the intensity of the part played by alliteration and assonance on occasion, let us examine two lines from Keats's "Ode to a Nightingale":

Charmed magic casements opening on the foam

Of perilous seas, in faery lands forlorn.

The assonance is indicated by dots and the alliteration by under-
lining; the different numbers of lines or dots indicates different
sound-groups. These two famous lines are rich in sound effects;
they are worth studying both for such obvious features as the repeated o's in "opening" and "foam" and the three f's, and also for
such things as (1) the progression in the relationship between the
different but similar *a* sounds in "charmed," "magic," and "casements"; (2) the successive deepening of the vowel sounds in the
last three words; (3) the general interweaving of the varieties of
assonantal and alliterative sounds; and (4) the predominant use of
smooth and long consonants and vowels, like *l* and *o*. It makes no
difference to the poem, by the way, if some of these sound effects
were produced unconsciously, or even accidentally; what matters is
that they are there to be perceived by a reader—or to have their
effect on him even without being clearly perceived.

RHYTHM AND METER

Allied to but different from the sound effects we have been discussing are rhythm and meter, both of which are concerned with
the time relationship between the sounds in literature rather than
with the sounds themselves.

Distinction between rhythm and meter. Our first duty in defining
rhythm and meter is to perceive clearly the relationship—and the
differences—between them. Rhythm, most fundamentally, is a series of beats or stresses occurring at regular intervals, the essential
element being the regularity. Meter is the regular, recurrent pat-
then of stressed and unstressed syllables in a line of poetry. Because it is regularly recurrent, this pattern is rhythmical, but meter
involves more than the rhythm it is based on; it involves, in most

English poetry, the number and the location of accented and unaccented syllables, and the relations between them.

For instance, consider the rhythm produced by beats a little less than a second apart. This we can find in the line, "But, soft! what light from yonder window breaks?" (Shakespeare, *Romeo and Juliet*). In a normal reading our voice will stress "soft," "light," "yon-," "win-," and "breaks," and these stresses will occur at intervals of a little less than a second. Thus we define the basic rhythm to some extent; but to describe the meter, we must add that before each stressed syllable there is one unstressed syllable, and that there are five beats to the line. If we analyze a line of a different meter in the same way, we will find, to begin with, that it may well have about the same basic rhythm as the iambic pentameter line from *Romeo and Juliet*. In "This is the forest primeval, the murmuring pines and the hemlock," (Longfellow, "Evangeline") the beats ("this," "for-," "-ev-," "mur-," "pines," "hem-") again occur a little less than a second apart; the noticeable difference in movement between the two lines is due not to a difference in basic rhythm but to a difference in meter. Longfellow's line is in dactylic hexameter, in which there are six beats to the line, each beat being *followed* by *two* unstressed syllables to produce a kind of waltz movement. In other words, meter produces variations of basic rhythms just the way a percussion instrument in a band does, by varying the relationship between stressed and unstressed sounds.

But we have been using the term "rhythm" in a very basic fashion. As it is usually used in the discussion of poetry—and prose— "rhythm" refers to more than the fundamental phenomenon. It is used to cover not only the rhythm basic to the meter, but also such things as the pace or tempo, the movement of the syntax and the sentence structure, and the relation of the sentence length to the line length. For example, both Pope's "Rape of the Lock" and Browning's "My Last Duchess" are written in iambic pentameter couplets, yet the difference in "rhythm" is more obvious than the similarity:

> What dire offence from amorous causes springs,
> What mighty contests rise from trivial things,
> I sing . . .
>   Say what strange motive, Goddess! could compel
> A well-bred lord to assault a gentle belle? . . .
>
>
> That's my last Duchess painted on the wall,
> Looking as if she were alive. I call
> That piece a wonder, now: Fra Pandolf's hands
> Worked busily a day, and there she stands. . . .

The lines from Browning's poem are less regular, more erratic in their rhythm, than Pope's lines, partly because of the run-on lines (those without a syntactical pause at the end; for example, ". . . I call / That piece . . ."), partly because of the more conversational phrasing, but mostly because of the striking rhetorical variations of the basic meter. Compare the actual metrical pattern of the first line of the poem ("Thát's mȳ lást Dúchēss páintēd ōn thē wáll") with that of normal iambic pentameter:

> (Browning): ′ — ′ ′ — ′ — — — ′
>
> (Normal):   — ′ — ′ — ′ — ′ — ′

Browning's line has the normal number of beats, at least according to this reading, but only three times do they coincide with the beats in a normal line—and there are other irregularities as well. The problem raised is often expressed thus: is this metrical? and consequently, is it poetical? The answer, as usual, is complex.

Perception of meter. To begin with, how do we readers determine whether a line is metrical or not, and if so, what the particular meter is? First, we read the line, and the rest of the poem, too, in order to hear what syllables the natural vocal stress falls on. Note that we read as if the lines were *prose;* we don't start out with a preconceived idea of what the rhythm should be, and try to force the lines into that pattern. It is not our job to create the rhythm of the lines, but the poet's, by his choice and placement of words and punctuation; if we read the lines normally—that is, pronouncing the words and weighting the punctuation the way the poet or anyone else would—the rhythm that the poet intended should emerge of its own accord. And it is precisely because that rhythm may be intentionally irregular at some points in the poem that we should not try to force a rhythmical pattern on a poem; if we do so, we will usually distort the normal pronunciation of at least some words.

For an illustration, try the experiment of first reading the lines from "My Last Duchess" just as if they were prose, and next, reading them according to a strict iambic rhythm. The "prose" reading will probably produce a rhythm something like this:

That's mȳ lást Dúchēss páintēd ōn t̄he wáll, / loókin̄g ās íf

s̄he wēre ālíve. Ī cáll / that̄ piéce ā wónder, ńow: Frā

Pándōlf's hánds / wórked búsilȳ ā dáy, and t̄here s̄he stánds.

When the lines are read, next, in strict iambic rhythm, there appear a number of distortions, the most obvious being the heavy stress on the second syllable in "looking." There is always some argument about what words in the lines would be stressed in a "normal" reading, but it is clear that these lines are not regularly iambic.

On the other hand, it is also clear that they are basically iambic, despite the irregularity. We find this out by reading enough of the poem to discover what the most common foot is and how many feet there are in most lines. In the first four lines of "My Last Duchess" there are more iambs than any other type of foot, and each line has five feet (though this might be argued for line 2); one line, the third, is perfectly regular iambic pentameter, thereby establishing the norm for the poem as a whole. Many later lines may be more or less irregular, but the iambic five-foot meter will be in evidence often enough to maintain itself as the basis for the poem;

and we can expect every line to show some evidence of the poem's basic meter. The amount of irregularity desirable—or permissible —will vary from poet to poet, and according to the literary conventions and traditions which govern a particular writer; there is no absolute rule. We can be sure of only two things: first, few poems are completely irregular, for in that case they would not usually be called poetry (meter generally being considered essential to verse); and second, few good poems are regular for any length of time, for such a lack of variety is painfully monotonous.

In taking the first step toward identifying the meter, then, we read the given poem almost as if it were prose; we expect it to be neither perfectly regular nor completely irregular. We note the usual—that is, the "normal"—number of syllables in the line, and the location of the stressed syllables in a normal line. Once we have done that, we are in a position to determine the pattern formed by the contrast between the accented and the unaccented syllables, that is, the meter.

The nature of the pattern depends largely on whether the stressed syllable is preceded or followed by an unstressed syllable and on how many unstressed syllables there are. This last is easy to determine once the accented syllables are identified; to answer the first question—to determine whether the meter "falls" or "rises"—we must examine the meter in more detail. The ideal line for scansion (analysis of meter) would be one in which each foot consisted of one word whose accent pattern was perfectly "normal" (a foot is the combination of stressed and unstressed syllables that constitutes the rhythmic unit of the line; for example, a word stressed — ′ is an iambic foot, and a word stressed ′ — is a trochaic foot). These lines are rare, but the following from John Masefield's "Cargoes" will illustrate: "Státelȳ Spánish gálleōns cóming from the Ísthmūs." All but the fifth foot are clearly and inherently trochaic; the line is trochaic hexameter. Similarly, the words "Sándalwōod, cédārwōod . . ." at the beginning of line 5 of "Cargoes" are clearly dactylic. It is more difficult to find perfect iambic lines, for

English words are not very often accented on the last syllable; in the first line of Shelley's "Remorse," however, two of the feet are iambic because of the inherent stress pattern of the words (*away* and *beneath*) while the other feet are almost as obviously iambic: "Āwáy! the moór īs dárk bēneáth the moón."

One indication of the shape of the metrical foot, then, is the natural pronunciation of the polysyllabic words in the line. But these are not always reliable, simply because poets rarely make a practice of aligning the words and the metrical feet rigidly. In the line "Past rúined Īliōn Helēn lives" (W. S. Landor, "Verse," line 1), the three central words are intrinsically trochaic, but the line is nevertheless iambic, as we see from a number of things. To begin with, we see that the other lines in the poem are predominantly iambic. The fourth line is obviously normal: "Īmmórtāl yóuth tō mórtāl máids." But what about the first line, which seems largely trochaic; can it fit into the rhythm of the rest of the poem? It can because of the stress pattern in the last two syllables, which is basically iambic, the beat coming on the final syllable, "lives." Once we perceive this iambic conclusion to the line, we can actually scan the whole line as regular iambic tetrameter: "Pāst rúined Īliōn Helēn líves." The unstressed syllables in "rúined," "Īliōn," and "Helēn" are the first half of an iamb rather than the second half of a trochee. Instead of coinciding with the normal stress of the separate words in the line, the metrical feet split the words down the middle—a common enough occurence.

There are many poems whose lines are not all metrically the same, like Frost's "Fire and Ice," and Masefield's "Cargoes." In these we cannot always identify a normal meter by examining several lines, but must deal with each line separately to some extent. There are various kinds of metrical differences between lines, some causing more difficulty in scansion, some less. The least troublesome—and the most common—is a simple difference in the number of feet: this is the case in "Fire and Ice," for instance, and in many ballads. This situation causes little difficulty because we can still check various lines and determine the basic type of foot, that which sets the general rhythm of the lines no matter what their length. When the lines differ in the basic type of foot, however, the scansion of irregular lines demands extra attention, especially if the type of foot changes from a "falling" one (trochee, dactyl) to a "rising" one or vice versa. For example, in "Cargoes," the first stanza reads as follows:

> Quínquiréme of/Nínevéh from/dístant/Óphir
> Rówing/hóme tó/háven/in súnny Pálestíne,
> Wíth a cárgo óf ívory,
> And ápes/ and péacocks,
> Sándalwóod,/ cédarwóod,/ and swéet/ white wíne.

The first line is trochaic hexameter (six feet); the second is also hexameter, but it is half trochaic, half iambic; and the third line is anapestic dimeter (two feet) with an extra syllable at the end—not to mention the other metrical peculiarities in lines 4 and 5. There can always be arguments about this scansion of the lines because of the metrical variety in the stanza. Yet we should note that these problems in scanning are to some degree academic. For instance, as long as we actually perceive the meter, reflect that perception in our reading and in our accent marks, it makes little real difference where we put the foot divisions. If we read the poem as it was written, allowing the words to produce the metrical movement intrinsic to the lines, and we can indicate that movement by our diagraming, our scansion will be adequate.

Our fundamental concerns with meter and rhythm in poetry should now be satisfied. An important thing to remember is that we should not expect every poem we read to be metrically neat and regular. Since we must have a certain degree of irregularity in any poem, we must expect anomalies now and then. But before we count them as outright defects, let us remind ourselves that there is still much to learn about meter, to begin with, and that what counts, ultimately, is the total effect of the rhythm and the meter and their relation to the other elements of the poem, rather than the academic purity and precision that we sometimes look for in poetry.

Rhythm in prose. So much for meter in poetry; how do we analyze the rhythm of prose—and, indeed, is prose rhythmical? Yes, it is, more or less, and the more regular the rhythm, the closer it comes to poetry; thus Conrad's prose is more poetic than Hardy's. Typically, the rhythm of prose—using "rhythm" in its most basic sense—is less regular than that of poetry; the accented syllables do not normally occur at intervals of the same length, as they do in poetry. Prose is not metrical, furthermore: the number and the pattern of stressed and unstressed syllables is not conventionally systematized, and there is thus less reason to scan prose. Although we can locate the accented and unaccented syllables, we can hardly identify the various metrical feet—and even if we could, we would not have any "normal" patterns with which to compare them. We do not expect prose to be written in iambic pentameter, for example, and complain when we find too many stresses in a row.

At the same time we must recognize that good prose is always somewhat rhythmical in a basic sense; the stressed and unstressed syllables occur in a more regular pattern than we might think offhand. If we scan a prose sentence by an accomplished writer, we find that the "meter" is not so different, after all, from that of poetry.

> I walked about on the shore, lifting up my hands
> And my whole being wrapt up in a contemplation
> Of my deliverance; making a thousand gestures
> And motions, which I cannot describe . . . .

This is from the first chapter of Daniel Defoe's *Robinson Crusoe,* and although the passage was not chosen completely at random, it is not especially "poetic" in general. Yet it is almost as rhythmical as the lines from "My Last Duchess" quoted earlier in prose form, or as Hamlet's soliloquy, as we can see if we write that as prose:

> To be, or not to be—that is the question: whether 'tis nobler in the mind to suffer the slings and arrows of outrageous fortune or to take arms against a sea of troubles, and by opposing end them.

The rhythm of prose varies in regularity from writer to writer; the style in our best newspapers, though competent, is hardly mellifluous, while at the other end of the scale the measured cadences of Sir Thomas Browne's *Urn-Burial* (1568) overlap those of poetry:

> And therefore restless inquietude for the diuternity of our memories unto present considerations, seems a vanity almost out of date, and superannuated piece of folly.

Rhythm in prose is more difficult to analyze than poetry for two general reasons. First, as far as the basic rhythm is concerned, prose is looser and more irregular than poetry, as we have noted; there are no objective standards with which it is expected to conform, so that we must analyze it in terms of its relationship with the other elements, such as the style, in a given passage. Second, because prose is not metrical, we define its rhythm usually in the more complex sense, as the product of variations in pitch, juncture, and pace, as well as stress. These concepts can also be employed fruitfully in the detailed analysis of poetic rhythm as we shall see; learning something about them is important to a knowledge of the subtleties and refinements of sound effects in literature.

SUBTLETIES AND REFINEMENTS

FUNCTIONS OF SOUND EFFECTS

Rime. In the first section of this chapter, we considered at some length the most common and familiar function of rime, the structural. There are other functions which we should now recognize. Some of the most important of these are to provide an interesting repetition of sounds, to satisfy convention, and to produce an impression of order or intensity.

A fundamental pleasure is derived from hearing interesting sounds repeated, especially when they are varied slightly in the process. The function of rime of providing such repetition is undoubtedly one of the most basic of all—so basic that we usually ignore it. It seems a rather simple-minded pleasure, yet it is probably the ultimate reason why rime was devised in the first place and then developed into a poetic convention. And this conventional aspect of rime is another important function of rime.

Rime has been used for a very long time by many poets. It seems at times almost inherent in poetry; when Shakespeare wrote, in Sonnet 55, "Not marble, nor the gilded monuments / Of princes, shall outlive this powerful rime . . ." he was using "rime" as a synonym for "poem," even though he used blank (that is, unrimed) verse in his plays. When we read poetry, we almost expect to find it rimed, and are faintly surprized if it is not. It seems strange to us that the earliest English poetry was never deliberately rimed. Instead its structure was based on alliteration, as we shall see shortly. After the Norman conquest, however, this practice died out, and since then rime has been an almost integral part of poetry. Like any other conventional device, rime may serve other purposes than mere decoration. It can, as we know, form part of the structure of a poem—but even if it does not, it will function effectively if it satisfies a convention. One side of man derives pleasure from familiar, traditional things: as a conventional technique, rime provides this pleasure.

Now we come to a more general function of rime, a function whose effects are pervasive and profound. The general effect of rime is to produce an impression of order and control, even of restraint. In order to perceive and appreciate this basic though intangible effect, students who are not sufficiently used to poetry will

need to develop deliberately their perception of their own attitudes. Let us consider the difference between the effect of Byron's
Don Juan, which is rimed, and Milton's *Paradise Lost,* which is
not:

> I want a hero: an uncommon want,
> When every year and month sends forth a new one,
> Till, after cloying the gazettes with cant,
> The age discovers he is not the true one;
> Of such as these I should not care to vaunt,
> I'll therefore take our ancient friend Don Juan . . . .
>
> (Canto I, ll. 1–6)

> Of man's first disobedience, and the fruit
> Of that forbidden tree, whose mortal taste
> Brought death into the world, and all our woe,
> With loss of Eden, till one greater Man
> Restore us, and regain the blissful seat,
> Sing, heavenly Muse . . . .
>
> (Bk. I, ll. 1–6)

Or Milton's "Lycidas" and Browning's "The Bishop Orders His
Tomb":

> . . . Lycidas is dead, dead ere his prime,
> Young Lycidas, and hath not left his peer.
> Who would not sing for Lycidas? he knew
> Himself to sing, and build the lofty rhyme.
> He must not float upon his watery bier
> Unwept, and welter to the parching wind,
> Without the meed of some melodious tear.
>
> (ll. 8–14)

> . . . I shall fill my slab of basalt there,
> And 'neath my tabernacle take my rest,
> With those nine columns round me, two and two,
> The odd one at my feet where Anselm stands:
> Peach-blossom marble all, the rare, the ripe
> As fresh-poured red wine of a mighty pulse.
>
> (ll. 23–30)

We can perceive in *Paradise Lost* and "The Bishop" a relative looseness or flow, an impression of flexibility due to their lack of rime. There is neatness and regularity suggested by rime that may suit one poem but not another.

This "intensity" produced by rime can be seem clearly—and artificially—in the occasional appearance of rime in a long un-rimed poem or in a blank-verse play. A number of Shakespeare's early plays contain rimed passages that stand out, for various purposes, because of their rime. In *Romeo and Juliet,* for instance, not only do many scenes end with rimed couplets for emphasis, but when the two young lovers first meet (Act 1, Scene 5), their dialogue takes the form of a sonnet:

> *Romeo:* If I profane with my unworthiest hand
> This holy shrine, the gentle fine is this:
> My lips, two blushing pilgrims, ready stand
> To smooth that rough touch with a tender kiss.
> *Juliet:* Good Pilgrim [Romeo is so costumed at the ball], you
> do wrong your hand too much,
> Which mannerly devotion shows in this:
> For saints [Juliet's costume] have hands that pilgrims'
> hands do touch,
>
> And palm to palm is holy palmers' [pilgrims'] kiss.
> *Romeo:* Have not saints lips, and holy palmers too?
> *Juliet:* Ay, pilgrim, lips that they must use in pray'r.
> *Romeo:* O, then, dear saint, let lips do what hands do!
> They pray; grant thou, lest faith turn to despair.
> *Juliet:* Saints do not move, though grant for prayers' sake.
> *Romeo:* Then move not while my prayer's effect I take.

Finally, we might raise the question of what the ultimate function of rime in general is. Certainly it provides us with a relatively simple pleasure in repeated sounds with the added refinement of such particular effects as emphasizing certain lines or phrases. It evidently also serves, however, like imagery and figurative language, to help us to participate in or perceive more immediately the experiences and ideas embodied in poetry. Or does it, on the contrary,

amount to a "distancing" device, forcing us in some measure to abstract ourselves from the raw material of literature in order to impose
a more abstract intellectual discipline on our conception of it; is it an
objective convention at the service of art? Rime can function in
different ways at different times, or even at the same time, but we
must always look behind the immediate effects of literary devices
in order to concern ourselves with the basic nature of literature.

Functions of other sound effects. Other sound effects besides
rime were defined and illustrated in the first half of this chapter.
Let us discuss now what purposes they serve, starting with one of
the less obvious functions, the *structural.*

We don't usually think of alliteration or assonance, and certainly
not onomatopoeia, as structural devices, but directly or indirectly
they may serve as such, as we have already seen. Specifically, assonance may constitute the basis for rimes that provide some of a
poem's structure, and alliteration too can still occasionally fulfill
that purpose, as in Richard Wilbur's "Junk":

> An axe angles
>   from my neighbor's ashcan;
> It is hell's handiwork,
>   the wood not hickory,
> The flow of the grain
>   not faithfully followed.

This poem is a modern emulation of the earliest English poetry.
For centuries alliteration was the backbone of English verse-form.
In the following passage, typically, the two halves of each line are
linked regularly by alliteration (rime, as we have noted, was not
used structurally). This is the beginning of the Old English epic,
Beowulf (c. 700), as translated by F. B. Gummere:

> Lo, praise of the powers of people-kings
> Of spear-armed Danes, in days long sped,
> We have heard, and what honor the athelings [princes] won!

Richard Wilbur's poem, a deliberate throwback to a supposedly
obsolete prosody, is testimony to the continued structural power of

alliteration. In more ordinary verse, at the same time, alliteration, and assonance, too, are still used pervasively enough to constitute a kind of structural element—a thread running through the verse —since coherence is a kind of structure.

The more obvious functions of alliteration, of assonance, and to some extent of onomatopoeia are the most important ones. Briefly and generally, these devices are used for coherence, for emphasis, and for tone or atmosphere. That is, alliteration and assonance establish links between words, thereby increasing the coherence in the line and emphasizing those words and the connection between them at the same time. Onomatopoeia, too, is used for emphasis by virtue of the clarity and immediacy of the sounds represented; "crash" is plainly more vivid than "the sound of breaking glass."

When we analyze the use of sounds for the development of tone and atmosphere we encounter a problem. We can feel the difference between sibilants (*s*'s and the like) and liquid consonants (*l*'s and *r*'s), and between broad or low vowels ($\bar{a}$, $\bar{o}$, $\bar{u}$) and sharp or high ones ($\breve{i}$, $\bar{e}$); we must for the sake of accuracy identify the effects of these sounds carefully, being neither too vaguely general nor too specific. It is inaccurate to say that *s*'s sound sinister, for example, or that long *o*'s are mournful—the effects are not that specific; nor can they be identified in isolation from the other elements of the particular work. At the same time, we should be more precise than to say that broad vowels and liquid consonants are simply longer or smoother than sibilants and sharp vowels. The most valid question to ask is "are the sounds consistent with the total character of the context?" For instance, consider Milton's use of "murmur" in line 9 of his sonnet "On His Blindness":

> When I consider how my light is spent . . .

> And that one talent which is death to hide
> Lodged with me useless . . .

> "Doth God exact day-labor, light denied?"
> I fondly ask. But Patience, to prevent
> That murmur, soon replies . . . .

What can we say about the sound of the word "murmur", which in other contexts has represented the sound of bees (" . . . murmuring of innumerable bees": Tennyson, "Come Down, O Maid") and of flies ("The murmurous haunt of flies on summer eves": Keats, "Ode to a Nightingale"), not to mention that of a gentle stream or a restless crowd of people? In isolation, the sound of the word has no specific inherent referent, while at the same time, it does have a general flavor that is adaptable to specific contexts: here, "murmur" reflects the tone of subdued and faintly sullen complaint that is evident throughout the context.

Before turning to meter and rhythm, we must note a few cases of relatively rare, though sometimes startlingly effective, sound devices. First, read the following lines aloud:

The hare limped trembling through the frozen grass . . . .
                          (Keats, "The Eve of St. Agnes")

When Ajax strives some rock's vast weight to throw . . . .
                          (Pope, "Essay on Criticism")

With hatefulest disrelish writhed their jaws . . . .
                          (Milton, *Paradise Lost,* Bk. X, 1. 569)

          . . . the unwieldy elephant,
          To make them mirth, used all his might, and wreathed
          His lithe proboscis . . . .
                          (*Paradise Lost,* Bk. IV, 11. 345–347)

In all of these cases, the sound seems "an echo to the sense," as Pope put it in the "Essay on Criticism," though not through onomatopoeia, alliteration, or assonance. In the first two cases, it is the difficulty of enunciating the words that produces the effect, while in the second two, the sounds of the letters and the actual sensation of pronouncing them are what count. These techniques, for which there is no common name (though "cacophony" is evident here—that is, unpleasant combinations of sounds) are perhaps close to onomatopoeia, although no sound is actually reproduced.

Such special effects as these will indicate the function of sound effects in general. In addition to functioning as part of the structure, sound effects almost inevitably serve to increase or intensify our participation in the experiences or ideas presented. They are much like, and in fact overlap with, auditory imagery, which we already know is a primary means of enabling us to perceive the material of a literary work immediately. When we recall that one function of rime—and, indeed, of prosodic conventions in general —is to increase the "psychological distance" between the reader and the raw material of the literary work, we realize that our position as readers is neatly ambiguous. For a work of art to be effective, it must allow—in fact, compel—the reader to perceive its material with a certain degree of immediacy; yet in order to *be* a work of art rather than merely a piece of undigested subject matter, it must impose on itself and its raw material some kind of objective and abstract discipline or perspective. The opposition of these two tendencies produces a tension that can never be completely resolved.

FUNCTIONS OF METER AND RHYTHM

Metrical irregularity. One way that this tension manifests itself in the prosody of a poem is in the relationship between the basic, normal meter and the almost inevitable irregularities. It is possible, of course, for a poem to be channeled and shaped strictly; that is, the words and phrases can be so tightly controlled that they fit into a given normal meter with no really significant variations. But this degree of discipline produces a mechanical and lifeless rigidity of rhythm. The poem will have the movement of this meter, but the movement will be imposed and artificial rather than "organic." For the rhythm to help us attain immediate contact with the material in a poem, it must emerge partly from the material itself and from ways of thinking and feeling about it that are not dictated by a purely literary convention.

This means that prosodic techniques will often be employed erratically in order to enhance the intrinsic character of the material.

Mechanical regularity in meter vitiates a literary work, while complete irregularity is not art; in the middle lies an area in which the tension between the two poles produces vitality.[1]

Let us examine briefly an example of the "counterpoint" between the metrical norm and the irregularity in a passage. Here is the beginning of Andrew Marvell's "To His Coy Mistress":

> Hád wē būt wórld ēnoúgh, ānd tíme,
>
> Thīs cóynēss, Lády, wére nō críme.
>
> Wé wōuld sīt dówn ānd thínk whích wáy
>
> Tō wálk ānd páss oūr lóng lóve's dáy.

The normal meter is determined plainly enough in the first two lines. The first foot in line 1 is a trochee instead of an iamb—a common type of "substitution" (replacement of a normal foot by a different one) for the beginning of a poem. By the time we reach the third and fourth lines, we are accustomed to, and expect, a particular metrical rhythm, iambic tetrameter. When we encounter the irregularities in those lines, therefore, they are superimposed on and contrast with our metrical habit and expectation. The stress patterns of the particular words in those lines are different from the pattern we carry in the back of our minds—that is how we realize, though no doubt unconsciously at first, that parts of those lines are irregular. And in the rest of the poem, we continue to be alternately reminded of our metrical habit on the one hand, and presented with variations of it on the other. The resulting tension, while often frustrating to unsophisticated readers, is an important source of a poem's vitality.

Variations in meter have other more specific effects as well. We can lump many of these together under the heading of "emphasis," but that is not a very informative term. What counts is what is

[1] See Aldous Huxley's comments on Poe's "Ulalume" in "Vulgarity in Literature," in *Collected Essays,* New York, 1958, for a witty and pertinent illustration of the difference between mechanical meter and "organic" variation.

emphasized, and how, and what kind of emphasis it is—and we encounter the same problem in answering these questions as when we try to identify the effect of various vowel and consonant sounds. Yet the result of substitutions is often sharply perceptible and effective. Notice, for example, the strong beats at the end of line 4 of Marvell's poem above; note how they slow down the tempo (in conjunction with the alliteration and the assonance) and echo, or reinforce, the sense of the passage. Similarly, notice how the pace is speeded up to emphasize the meaning, by the dactyls in line 22 of the same poem: "Time's winged chariot hurrying near." By setting aside for the moment the normal meter and introducing particular patterns of beats and offbeats to suit particular passages, poets develop "organically" the flow of ideas and experiences instead of leaving it at the mercy of a perfectly rigid verse form.

Analysis of rhythm. The foregoing discussion of meter may make it seem very complex, and the process of analyzing it even more so. But, as a matter of fact, the conception of rhythm embodied in traditional metrics is very limited. What is needed is the precision of linguistic analysis to indicate accurately and in detail the genuine complexites of poetic and prose rhythms; for this, the traditional concepts of English metrics are too few and too simple.

We turn first to linguistics in order to deal with the fact that there are actually several degrees of stress or heaviness of accent, rather than only the two distinguished by traditional metrics (the beat and the offbeat, as in the word "méter"). Most modern linguists believe that four different degrees can be clearly distinguished (these are customarily called primary, secondary, tertiary, and weak; and they are represented by the symbols ´, ^, `, and ˅). Consider, for instance, the different degrees of stress in "April is the cruelest month/ . . ." (T. S. Eliot, "The Waste Land," l. 1).

Further, linguistic analysis enables us to distinguish the many and varied pauses or breaks in the flow of language (called "junctures"). Only some of these can be represented by conventional punctuation or by such terms as "run-on line" and "caesura." For precision, we use the linguists' identification of four different kinds of juncture, as exemplified here with the juncture symbols in parentheses: (1) night (+) rate [contrast this with the lack of juncture in "nitrate"]; (2) "After great pain (→) a formal feeling comes"; (3) "My heart aches, (↗) and a drowsy numbness . . ."; (4) "Then all smiles stopped together. (↘) There she stands. . . ."

Finally, traditional metrics takes little account of variations in pitch beyond noting the difference between lower and higher vowels ("tomb" versus "team"). Pitch, and the variation of it, helps determine the whole tone and meaning of a passage. More to the point right now, it can suggest or encourage a given rhythm—low tones seem to imply a slower rhythm than high ones—and by influencing juncture and stress it can affect the rhythm more particularly. The relationship between these elements is complex, but the fact that pitch can affect the others may be illustrated by considering the difference in rhythm between the following readings of a line from Shakespeare's Sonnet 129 (degrees of pitch are here numbered from low to high):

The first reading establishes a climactic order in the three epithets, and presents "full of blame" as a final climax adding another fault —a new kind—to the list. The second reading, on the other hand, presents the three epithets as equal items in a list, and uses the final phrase "full of blame" as a concluding emphatic summary of the consequences. We might also note that both of these readings are permitted by the meter; the fact emerges clearly that there can be a considerable difference between meter and its ordinary variations on the one hand and the actual readings of a work on the other.

If analyzing the strictly metrical variations in a poem is a long and difficult task, it is obviously going to be even more laborious to analyze fully any given reading of prose or of poetry. It can be, and has been, done for short poems, however, and it is a rewarding process. We might attempt it with the first line of Hamlet's famous soliloquy:

This annotation is much more complex than metrical scansion. But it is not the notations that are complex; it is the linguistic elements that they represent and which form the flow, the rhythm of the language. Although metrical analysis helps us understand the conventional foundation of poetic rhythm, only some kind of linguistic analysis will enable us to define the "organic" rhythm of poetry—or prose. That analysis is thus especially helpful in clarifying the complex rhythms of prose. In poetry it leads to an understanding of the fluid variations in the relationship between the rhythm and the meter which can constitute such an important characteristic of the form.

Before closing this discussion of meter and rhythm, we should make two final qualifications. First, not all poetry—even all English poetry—is metrical; and second, the literary concept of "rhythm" sometimes includes other things than the flow of language.

Much poetry in foreign languages is nonmetrical, or metrical in a different way from ours. But a good deal of poetry written in English is not based on conventional metrics. Old English poetry, and some Middle English alliterative verse is almost exclusively accentual, little attention having been paid to unstressed syllables. The "sprung rhythm" of Gerard Manley Hopkins, in the nineteenth century, was similarly based almost exclusively on stressed syllables; the following lines from "The Windhover" are analogous to iambic pentameter:

I cáught this mórning mórning's mínion, kíng-

dom of dáylight's dáuphin, dápple-dawn-drawn Fálcon, in

his ríding

Of the rólling lével undernéath him steady áir, and

stríding . . . .

A metrical and rhythmical analysis of this poetry is a real chal-
lenge! In addition, what we call "free verse" is nonmetrical—
though that does not mean that the poetry of Whitman or Sand-
burg, for example, is not rhythmical. Its rhythm is more irregular
than most conventional verse and is therefore closer to that of
prose:

When lilacs last in the dooryard bloom'd,
And the great star early droop'd in the western sky
in the night,
I mourn'd, and yet shall mourn with ever-returning spring.
(Whitman)

Second, "rhythm" in literature almost always means language
rhythm, and usually connotes verse, but it has been used—somewhat metaphorically perhaps—to refer to such things as the
succession of incident in a narrative and the progression of the
conflict in a plot in such phrases as "the rhythm of the narrative"
or "of the plot." There are other ways in which almost all of the
terms we are concerned with have been used, but we should distinguish between common and recognized usage and occasional metaphorical usage.

5   ❦❦❦❦❦❦❦❦❦❦❦

Style

Style in literature as in any other art refers to the artist's way of doing things. It can be a very general concept including several literary qualities that we have already discussed, in particular the verbal ones such as rhythm and figurative language. Those concepts were so complex and important that we had to consider them separately, but we should remember that they belong logically in the same category as the stylistic concepts we are going to discuss now: diction, sentence structure, allusion, ambiguity, irony, paradox, and tone.

BASIC TERMS AND CONCEPTS

DICTION

Diction, briefly, is choice of words. The difference between "Of man's first disobedience . . ." and "With regard to mankind's initial insubordination . . ." is one of diction. Obviously an important element of style, diction can vary in several ways.

To begin with, it makes a great deal of difference to literary style whether the words used are predominantly long or short. The effect of a multitude of polysyllables differs markedly from that of a lot of short words. Long words seem to slow down the pace and make the style heavier, generally speaking, although other variable elements—such as the concreteness of the diction—can modify this effect. But certainly Sir Thomas Browne, and Milton to some extent, are known for their use of long words, while A. E. Housman and Hemingway tend to use short ones (for all of these, see Chapter 4).

But it is difficult to find writers whose diction is thoroughly characterized by long or short words; most writers' diction varies considerably in this respect, depending on their themes, subject matter, and circumstances. Browne, for instance, more often employs long words in his *Urn-Burial,* from which the example of prose rhythm in Chapter 4 was taken, than he did in his less philosophical and meditative *Religio Medici:* "Now for my life, it is a miracle of thirty years, which to relate were not a history, but a piece of poetry. . . ." Similarly, Shakespeare for one scene writes, "The multitudinous seas incarnadine . . ." (*Macbeth,* Act II, scene 2), while in another he reduces Hamlet's problem to the monosyllables, "To be or not to be . . ." (Act III, scene 1). What is important in our consideration of style is not so much which writers use long words or short ones, but when these are used and what the result is.

Another way in which diction varies is in the familiarity of the words. At one extreme are the archaisms ("wain" for "wagon"), the poeticisms ("o'er"), the technical and specialized words (the nautical and whaling vocabulary in *Moby-Dick*)—all the words not widely known to readers, or at least not often seen or used by them. At the other extreme is the vocabulary common to all English-speaking men, women, and children. The question of how far to go in either direction has been answered differently at different times. In *The Faerie Queene* (1590, 1595) Spenser deliberately adopted an archaic diction to suit the "antiquated" subject of knight-errantry. In the eighteenth century, the desire to achieve elevation and generality in poetry sometimes resulted in an attempt to avoid "specialized" or "technical" words, by the use of such generalized terms as "finny tribe" (for "fishes"), and "his rural seat" for the place in the countryside where a cuckoo is found (Michael Bruce, "To the Cuckoo").

In revolt against this kind of artificial diction, William Wordsworth argued for poetry written "in a selection of language really used by men" (Preface to *Lyrical Ballads,* 1800), and although he did not restrict himself to a perfectly common vocabulary his diction helped make his poetry refreshingly direct and down-to-earth. The real question, after all, is not whether common or esoteric language is appropriate to poetry in general, but what diction is appropriate to particular works: *Paradise Lost* could hardly have been written exclusively in "language really used by men," while Chaucer could not have written *The Canterbury Tales* in high-flown, "poetic" diction, for most of them are supposedly told by very common or ordinary people.

In prose literature the question applies equally well though the variety of answers has not been quite as striking. There is a considerable difference in the familiarity of the diction between Dickens and Hemingway on the one hand, who were writing for a wide audience that could not be expected to be familiar with recondite language, and Sir Thomas Browne and Milton, who were aiming at a more highly educated audience; the language of James Joyce's *Ulysses* and of other impressionistic or stream-of-consciousness works raises special problems of familiarity that we will have to touch on later. And before we pass on we should remember not to oversimplify the problem by reducing it to whether the diction is common or unusual. Not all "unusual" diction is unusual in the same way, and it makes a great deal of difference to a work whether the diction is technical, or archaic, or simply polysyllabic. The differences between these kinds of diction are often just as great as those between the two extremes of familiarity.

The last general variation in diction to mention now is the etymological. As most of us know, the source of most English words is Latin on the one hand and Old English (Anglo-Saxon) on the other, the proportion being something like 70 percent to 25 percent. Though the words of Old English derivation account for only a quarter of the total vocabulary, those words are the ones we use most commonly: articles, pronouns, and connectives, and the "everyday" words like *man, girl, book, friend, eat, read,* and *write.* The Latinate words embody less ordinary things and concepts, or express finer shades of meaning, although many times we can express the same thing in either Old English derivatives or Latin derivatives (for example, *say* or *express; fourth* or *quarter; understand* or *comprehend*).

Characteristic differences between a Latinate diction and an Anglo-Saxon diction should now be easy to perceive. A Latinate vocabulary appears more elegant and subtle, yet is occasionally ponderous; Anglo-Saxon words seem plain and strong, but sometimes they may be too simple (note the difference between the diction of these two clauses). At the same time, Latinate words are usually longer and more formal than Anglo-Saxon words. Whether a particular writer deliberately elects to use one vocabulary or the other, or whether this choice is more nearly unconscious, is hard to say. In any case, the choice would most likely be based not so much on the etymology itself as on its result, the present character and function of the words. Consider the two passages from *Paradise Lost* which follow; the larger proportion of Latinate words in the lines from Book II is no doubt due to Milton's wish to heighten the style at that point. In Eve's words to Adam, from Book IV, the simplicity of the speaker and of what she says makes a commonplace—and therefore Anglo-Saxon—vocabulary more appropriate; the Latinate words are italicized:

High on a throne of *royal state,* which far
Outshone the wealth of Ormus and of Ind,
Or where the *gorgeous* East with richest hand
Showers on her kings *barbaric* pearl and gold,
Satan *exalted* sat, by *merit* raised
To that bad *eminence;* and, from *despair*
Thus high uplifted beyond hope, *aspires*
Beyond thus high, *insatiate* to *pursue*
Vain war with Heaven; and by *success* untaught,
His *proud imaginations* thus *displayed*. . .
                         (Bk. II, ll. 1–10)

To whom thus Eve *replied:* "O thou for whom
And from whom I was *formed* flesh of thy flesh,
And without whom I am to no end, my *guide*
And head! what thou hast said is *just* and right.
For we to him, indeed, all *praises* owe,
And daily thanks—I *chiefly,* who enjoy
So far the happier lot, *enjoying* thee
Preeminent by so much odds, while thou
Like *consort* to thyself canst nowhere find. . . ."
                         (Bk. IV, ll. 440–448)

As is the case with long or short words, writers whose diction is
predominantly of one derivation are rare. Our most common critical problem here is to observe how much the derivation of the vocabulary accounts for the character of the diction in particular
works or particular passages. In line 10 of Stephen Spender's "Express," for another example, there occurs a Latinate word which
could easily be supplanted by an Anglo-Saxon equivalent; contrast
the two versions:

The luminous self-possession of ships on ocean.

The shining self-possession of ships on ocean.

The Anglo-Saxon "shining" is vivid, and it even alliterates with
other words in the line, yet it is not as good as "luminous." The
difference is partly in the lower intensity of the Latinate word,

"shining" being too bright, partly in the more mellifluous sound of "luminous," and partly even in the word's Latinate flavor due to the syllables *lu-* and *-ous*.

SENTENCE STRUCTURE

Diction by itself is important to style, but we must remember as always that such elements interact within a wider context. Now, therefore, we must consider the structure of the sentences in which the words appear. Although we cannot review all the possible varieties of sentence structure—the various possible locations of adjectives and adverbs, for instance—we should note the main general differences.

Sheer length, to begin with, has a significant stylistic effect here as well as in diction. No matter how they are constructed, longer sentences generally seem more leisurely, more meditative than shorter ones. It is surprizingly easy to find contrasting examples of extremes: Hemingway and Henry James in American literature (see below for quotations), and in poetry Milton and Robert Herrick (for sentence length helps determine poetic style as well as prose style). As a matter of fact, this contrast between Milton and Herrick is particularly notable: Milton is renowned partly for the sustained, cumulative, on-rolling sentences we have seen above, while much of Herrick's charm is due to his neat brevity:

> Gather ye rose-buds while ye may,
>   Old Time is still a-flying;
> And this same flower that smiles to-day
>   Tomorrow will be dying.
>
>   ("To the Virgins, to Make Much of Time," ll. 1–4)

Even a cursory analysis of the Herrick and Milton passages, however, reveals that the sentences differ in more than length: they illustrate a number of other basic variations of sentence structure.

For one thing, the sentence from Book II of *Paradise Lost* is "periodic," at least down to "sat" in line 5, while Herrick's is "loose." That is, the principal statement in Milton's sentence is led up to as a climax, whereas in Herrick, the main meaning is used as a point of departure and is followed by reasons and consequences. Very often, as here, this means that in a periodic sentence the main clause comes at the end of the sentence, while in a loose sentence it comes at the beginning. The difference in effect is usually easy to apprehend: the loose construction, the normal one in English, seems more natural and casual, and sometimes it can seem disorganized; the periodic structure seems dignified, often dramatic, and sometimes stilted or ponderous. The effect will depend partly on the length of the sentence, of course, and on other stylistic features, too.

Another difference between Milton's and Herrick's sentences is that Milton's are more complicated in structure. Milton tends to rely more heavily on compound-complex sentence structure while Herrick leans toward simpler construction. Especially notable is the way modifying clauses and phrases interwoven around the main clause in Milton contrast with the simple forms of the statements in Herrick.

To conclude our discussion of sentence structure, let us refer again to Hemingway and Henry James. They contrast in almost every basic aspect of sentence structure, Hemingway tending toward short, simple, loose sentences, while James tends toward long and complex periods, as the following examples suggest:

> He was an old man who fished alone in a skiff in the Gulf Stream and he had gone eighty-four days now without taking a fish. In the first forty days a boy had been with him. But after forty days without a fish the boy's parents had told him that the old man was now definitely and finally *salao,* which is the worst form of unlucky, and the boy had gone at their orders in another boat which caught three good fish the first week . . . .
>
> (from *The Old Man and the Sea*)

> The story had held us, round the fire, sufficiently breathless, but except the obvious remark that it was gruesome, as, on Christmas

eve in an old house, a strange tale should essentially be, I remember no comment uttered till somebody happened to say that it was the only case he had met in which such a visitation had fallen on a child. The case, I may mention, was that of an apparition in just such an old house as had gathered us for the occasion—an appearance, of a dreadful kind, to a little boy sleeping in the room with his mother and waking her up in the terror of it; waking her not to dissipate his dread and soothe him to sleep again, but to encounter also, herself, before she had succeeded in doing so, the same sight that had shaken him . . . .

(from "The Turn of the Screw")

The striking dissimilarity between the styles of these two writers should not lead us to think that sentence structure is an either–or proposition. There are many combinations and permutations of the basic aspects of sentence structure, to begin with, so that it is difficult to pigeonhole writers neatly; and secondly, most writers avoid going to any stylistic extreme and therefore belong somewhere in the middle. Although we find examples of extremes easily enough, that does not mean that all writers belong in one camp or the other. As usual, the situation is not that simple. Our principal problem is to perceive the significance of the sentence structure in particular works or specific passages.

ALLUSION

The next stylistic concept to be considered, that of allusion, is different from diction and sentence structure, for it is not an integral element of style, but an optional device, an additional refinement. Very few writers actually wish to—or could, even if they did wish to—avoid allusion. An allusion is a mention of or reference to something, such as a character, an event, or a phrase, from a different literary work or from some different context. By such references a writer reveals the content of his mind, the literary and other knowledge stored there which is part of him and can hardly be set aside while he writes. Even if he could set it aside, he rarely would wish to, for allusions are one of the principal means of enriching a literary work by bringing to bear on it the associations and meanings connected with other works, and of placing it in a kind of perspective by relating it to the cultural tradition behind it.

The first critical problem for us is that of quantity, of the number of allusions. This quantity varies, practically speaking, from a total lack of specific references to the degree of allusiveness that so many students object to on first reading *Paradise Lost* or T. S. Eliot's *The Waste Land*. Such objections may seem irreverent, and they usually are—fortunately—but they are far from pointless, for the number of allusions a work contains is some indication of its originality. Though no literary work is completely derivative, nor completely original, a work that is highly allusive is more closely related to its cultural antecedents than one that lacks specific allusions. In this sense *Paradise Lost* is less original than, say, "Stopping by Woods on a Snowy Evening." Frost alludes only to the purported owner of the woods; he lives in the village, and that is all we need to know. Milton, on the other hand, depends very heavily on allusions, like those to Ormus and India in the lines quoted above from Book II, many of which are not self-explanatory. There are different kinds of originality, however, and different ways of achieving it; a highly allusive work may be very original in essence—or it may be deeply colored by tradition without being derivative, *Paradise Lost* being a case in point.

The sheer number of separate references is not always as important as the "weight" of the allusions. In Keats's "Eve of St. Agnes," for example, there is one basic allusion—an unstated one —to *Romeo and Juliet:* Keats's poem is the story of two young lovers who are united despite their feuding families. The analogy between the two works is so persistently evident that we can consider the poem profoundly if not multitudinously allusive.

In addition to the number and the weight of the allusions in a given work, we must consider the actual nature of the material alluded to, for this too makes a great deal of difference to a writer's style. Are the allusions primarily literary, or historical, or personal, or are they not thus restricted? Are they to current works, events, and persons, or to material from the past? And on the whole is the material alluded to widely familiar, or is it "private" or esoteric? The answers to these kinds of questions are important partly because they reveal something of the writer's mind, but principally because they reflect the character of the work itself and its impression on readers.

A work in which allusions are made to a variety of fields—politics and science, perhaps, as well as literature and history—may seem wider in scope and outlook than one in which the allusions are limited (we might contrast the breadth of Milton's work with the restriction of Keats's on this score). A work whose allusions are mainly to current things and events may seem fresh and lively, although those allusions (and the work) can quickly become dated if those current events are narrowly limited or temporary. Most important, at least for new readers of a given work, is the question of the familiarity of the material. If a writer alludes to material unfamiliar to the majority of readers, either because it is too private or too esoteric, or because our culture has changed over the centuries (as with Milton), his work may seem too obscure. Yeats's famous poem "Sailing to Byzantium" certainly alludes to a rather private symbolic process in the lines

> O sages standing in God's holy fire
> As in the gold mosaic of a wall,
> Come from the holy fire, perne in a gyre
> And be the singing-masters of my soul.

The phrase "perne in a gyre" evidently means something like "spin in a rising, whirling movement" (rather like a whirling dervish), but we can comprehend this only after learning something about the poet's private conception of experience. Then, in T. S. Eliot's *The Waste Land,* we find references to ancient Egyptian fertility rituals and to Medieval French "Romances" (narratives of knights and their deeds); these were certainly esoteric at the time the poem first appeared. In cases like these and Milton's, the allusions may seem to be largely wasted at first. Fortunately, scholars go to considerable lengths to clarify obscure allusions for us in footnotes, and through these we can achieve much of the satisfaction of recognizing an allusion.

Allusion presents writers with a dilemma: it can frustrate readers or it can offer them much insight. If allusions are too obscure, they will not simply fail to reach many readers, but will actually deter them. And if they are too numerous or too heavily weighted, they will make tradition a burden rather than a bulwark. On the other hand, allusions can achieve a great deal, economically, as does T. S. Eliot's "No! I am not Prince Hamlet . . ." in "The Love Song of J. Alfred Prufrock." The narrator in that poem, Prufrock, is quite like Hamlet in his indecisiveness and introspection, but he is far less important a person, being almost ridiculous compared to the Prince: all this, and more, is conveyed by those few words in the poem.

SPECIAL EFFECTS: AMBIGUITY, PARADOX, IRONY

Next, in still a different category from diction, sentence structure, and allusion, appear certain "secondary" stylistic effects that result from the elements of style already considered (and others, too, of course). These particular special effects, grouped because they all involve some kind of deliberate distortion or duplicity of meaning, are ambiguity, irony, and paradox. Briefly, ambiguity is the property of meaning two or more different things at the same time, irony is that of expressing one thing while making it clear that the opposite is meant, and paradox is apparent self-contradiction or deliberate inconsistency. We are now concerned with style, and will therefore deal with these special effects as they are manifested verbally; elsewhere—under "tragic irony," for instance—we will touch on their "situational" appearance.

Although the title of William Empson's famous book on the subject is *Seven Types of Ambiguity*,[1] we may here content ourselves with only two basic types. The first, the "either–or" kind, as it has been called, we are for good reasons taught to avoid; this ambiguity consists of saying something that can mean either of two incompatible things. For example, a student who writes "the size of the chair was unusual" might mean either unusually large or unusually small; the imprecision of the statement makes it impossible for us to tell which meaning was intended. Similarly, the Delphic oracle's statement that if Croesus waged war on Cyrus, he would destroy a great empire, was equally ambiguous; Croesus took "empire" to mean Cyrus', but it actually meant Croesus' own. This kind of puzzling ambiguity due to vagueness is obviously undesirable in most writing.

The other basic type of ambiguity, often highly desirable, involves two or more meanings, but these, though different, are perfectly compatible. It is possible in many cases to make statements that mean two or more different things all of which are related and all perfectly valid and pertinent. For example, in Milton's reference at the beginning of *Paradise Lost* to the first "mortal taste" of the apple, the word "mortal" can mean both "by a human being" and "deadly," and both meanings are relevant and appropriate. Similarly, the line "I have measured out my life with coffee spoons," in Eliot's "Prufrock" can mean both that the speaker could measure his life according to the number of teaparties and the like that he has attended, and that he has led a piddling, uneventful life, never having done anything dynamic or magnificent. And Conrad's title, *Heart of Darkness,* refers to the center of Africa ("the dark continent"), to the barbarism at that center, and to the savagery of the human heart in general, all of which are fundamental preoccupations of the novel.

This kind of ambiguity, instead of leaving the meaning uncertain

[1] London, 1930.

and unclear, makes for a richness and complexity that we appreciate more fully the more we perceive and understand it. Admittedly, this multiplicity of meaning or "plurisignation," as it is called by some critics, confuses some unsophisticated readers as well as those who insist on simplicity and clarity above all. Many students feel at first that this kind of serious punning contravenes their training in precision of expression because they fail to distinguish between the two basic kinds of ambiguity; at the same time, they ask, "Did the author intend all these meanings?" whereas the question should be, "Are these different meanings all valid and significant?" It is not what the writer intended to "put into" his work that counts, as far as the work itself is concerned, but what is actually there to be generally perceived.

Verbal paradox, next, like ambiguity, is a negation of clear and simple exposition. It is a statement that seems to contradict itself or seems inherently inconsistent. Milton's description of the illumination in hell as "darkness visible" (*Paradise Lost,* Bk. I, 1. 63) and his further statement that there ". . . hope never comes / That comes to all . . ." (ll. 66-67) are paradoxical. Often—many critics would say "usually"—paradox is a device of wit, a means of startling and amusing readers, although this entertainment serves to emphasize the truth (or half-truth) contained in the paradox. Oscar Wilde and George Bernard Shaw were masters of this half-light, half-serious witticism; Wilde's play *The Importance of Being Earnest* contains many paradoxes, such as these from Act I:

> Oh! it is absurd to have a hard and fast rule about what one should read and what one shouldn't. More than half of modern culture depends on what one shouldn't read.

> It is awfully hard work doing nothing. However, I don't mind hard work where there is no definite object of any kind.

> The amount of women in London who flirt with their own husbands is perfectly scandalous. It looks so bad. It is simply washing one's clean linen in public.

In G. B. Shaw's plays we find similar, though rather more pointed, examples:

> . . . The formation of a young lady's mind and character usually consists in telling her lies. . . .
>
> *(Man and Superman,* Act II)

> There are two tragedies in life. One is to lose your heart's desire. The other is to gain it.
>
> (Act IV)

Like most other literary devices or elements, paradox varies considerably in several ways. We have seen how it can be relatively light and amusing or serious and significant. It can also be brief or extended, of course, and casual or central: Milton's "darkness visible" is brief and casual (though significant), whereas in John Donne's "Valediction: Forbidding Mourning" we find a paradox developed through four entire stanzas as the climax to the main point of the poem: in line 21, Donne states that his and his wife's two separate souls are nevertheless one, and in the rest of the poem he explains this paradoxical relationship and its consequences by comparing their souls first to a sheet of gold foil, then, as we observed when discussing metaphor, to the legs of a draughtsman's compass:

> Our two souls, therefore, which are one,
>   Though I must go, endure not yet
> A breach, but an expansion,
>   Like gold to airy thinness beat.

> If they be two, they are two so
>   As stiff twin compasses are two;
> Thy soul, the fixed foot, makes no show
>   To move, but doth if the other do.

> And though it in the centre sit,
>   Yet, when the other far doth roam,
> It leans, and hearkens after it,
>   And grows erect as that comes home.

Such wilt thou be to me, who must
Like the other foot obliquely run:
Thy firmness makes my circle just,
And makes me end where I begun.

Finally, paradox can vary in "depth." It can sometimes be a mere trick of phrasing, inconsistent words artifically yoked together: "I feed me in sorrow and laugh in all my pain: / Likewise displeaseth me both death and life; / And my delight is causer of my pain" (Sir Thomas Wyatt, "Description of the Contrarious Passions in a Lover") while on the other hand it can concern problems or phenomena that have disturbed men profoundly. At this level, especially, it becomes difficult to draw the line between verbal paradox (expressed in words) and situational paradox. For instance, in *Oedipus,* the ordinarily sharp-eyed and sharp-witted king is "blind" to the horror of his situation (and in contrast, the blind prophet Tiresias can "see" the situation clearly). Oedipus' "blindness" is certainly a profound and pervasive paradox in the play. It is situational, of course, and at the same time it is verbalized periodically, as when Tiresias says to Oedipus: "Since you have taunted me with being blind, here is my word for you. / You have your eyes but see not where you are in sin, nor where you live, nor whom you live with." Profound situational paradox does not have to be put into words to be perceived in a literary work, but it usually is, in some fashion.

There is a good deal of similarity between paradox and irony because they both involve an opposition in logic between two or more elements. In paradox, the opposition is that of inconsistency or contradiction, while in irony it stems from a difference between appearance and reality—between what a writer says (that is, appears to mean) and what he actually means, verbal irony consisting in saying one thing in order to express the opposite: "What a gorgeous day!" as a comment on a dark and drizzly November morning is a clear example of simple irony. Though most verbal irony is not that simple or clear-cut, the basic elements are the same. In "A

Modest Proposal," for instance, Jonathan Swift expressed his sympathy for the poverty-stricken Irish and his hatred of their English oppressors by suggesting that the children of the Irish poor be sold for food. Swift does not say exactly the opposite of what he means, but what he does say implies a state of mind totally opposite to his real feelings, so that the basic contrast between what is said and what is meant emerges.

Swift's "Modest Proposal" is a notable example of verbal irony for a number of reasons, one of which is Swift's handling of a basic problem in irony, that of its obviousness. The problem is this: if the ironic intent (the fact that the author actually means the reverse of what he says) is not obvious enough, most readers will get a completely false impression of the purpose of the work, taking the apparent meaning seriously. If, on the other hand, the irony is too obvious, most readers will feel that they are being treated like children, that their intelligence is being insulted. Somewhere between these two extremes, which vary according to the particular work and indeed the particular reader, lies the area of effective verbal irony. Swift's solution to the problem was to adopt a very serious tone, to sound rational and straightforward—and yet sympathetic—so that we can take the work seriously at first (except perhaps for an occasional disturbing expression like "a child dropped from its dam," or "two hundred thousand couple whose wives are breeders"). Then, when he has practically convinced us of his sincerity, he presents his horrifying solution to Ireland's poverty, working out the details in a precise and reasonable tone: ". . . a well-grown, fat yearling child . . . roasted whole will make a considerable figure at a Lord Mayor's feast, or any other public entertainment." It is only late in the essay that the tone changes to bitterness and makes it obvious the author protests too much and definitely cannot be serious.

The tone of a literary work—that is, the reflection in it of the author's attitude toward his material, his audience, and himself—is a controlling factor in verbal irony. The nature and the effect of an ironical work depend both on the contrast between appearance and reality and also on how that contrast is brought out, how much it is emphasized, how seriously it is treated, and other aspects of tone. As with paradox, the lightness or seriousness of the irony depends on the tone in which it is expressed. There are, in fact, certain names for different kinds of irony, depending on the tone. Sarcasm, for example, is bitter personal irony close to insult or invective. When "mockery" is used to describe a kind of irony, that irony is usually gentler than sarcasm, although there are various degrees of violence possible here. Understatement, when it is ironical ("not bad" to mean "very good"), is obviously restrained in tone. Since most tonal varieties of irony have no particular name, however, we describe them directly as gentle, or bitter, or in some similar way. The point to note is that such differences exist because of differences in tone. "A Modest Proposal" and Pope's "The Rape of the Lock" are both ironical, but the bitter tone of the former is very different from the lightness and urbanity of the latter. We will discuss this kind of difference further when considering satire.

TONE

Tone does much more than determine the flavor of irony; indeed, it is crucial and pervasive in a literary work. As the author's evident attitude toward his work, his audience, and himself, it can be more than merely important to a work; it can be central to its meaning. Just as the tone of a speaker's voice can often determine whether an expression is a deadly insult or an expression of friendship, the tone of a literary work will indicate just how we are to approach it. We would read "The Secret Life of Walter Mitty" differently from the way we would read "The Short Happy Life of Francis Macomber," because there is a profound general difference in tone between comedy and tragedy. Similarly, but more subtly, we would not read one of Dickens' serious novels such as *David Copperfield* or *A Tale of Two Cities* and Shakespeare's *Macbeth* in the same way. It is somewhat difficult to speak of the tone in a play as a matter of style, because the particular tone varies according to the character speaking and the scene, but we can perceive that Dickens' works are more sentimental and a little less intense than *Macbeth,* and for this reason we approach them differently, reading Dickens more nearly for pure entertainment. Varieties of tone, though often subtle and complex to distinguish in detail, can be satisfactorily identified in general terms. We can identify broadly a conversational or a rhetorical tone, a flat or a dramatic or a lyrical tone, a personal or an impersonal tone, and so on. Then, once that preliminary step has been taken, we must do justice to the usually complex overtones of a literary work, and indicate the often extremely significant variations in tone within the work.

Tone, and especially changes in tone, are to be noted in restricted literary contexts as well as in large ones like a whole play or novel. Tone is general in that it is the product usually of a number of stylistic elements rather than being a specific element itself; indeed, it can be defined as the emotional effect of any or all of the elements of style, not to mention the interaction of style, subject matter, and theme. But this effect can be felt within narrow limits and can change quickly and radically on occasion, as we can see from Shakespeare's Sonnet 29, "When in Disgrace with Fortune and Men's Eyes."

> When, in disgrace with fortune and men's eyes,
> I all alone beweep my outcast state,
> And trouble deaf heaven with my bootless cries,
> And look upon myself and curse my fate,
> Wishing me like to one more rich in hope,
> Featur'd like him, like him with friends possess'd,
> Desiring this man's art, and that man's scope,
> With what I most enjoy contented least;
> Yet in these thoughts myself almost despising,
> Haply I think on thee, and then my state,
> Like to the lark at break of day arising
> From sullen earth, sings hymns at heaven's gate;
> For thy sweet love rememb'red such wealth brings
> That then I scorn to change my state with kings.

In the octave, the tone is melancholy, even despairing, and perhaps a little self-pitying; we could add other adjectives to help us describe precisely the particular flavor of the tone. We can identify the tone most precisely by picking out the stylistic features that produce it. Some of these are key words like "disgrace," "bootless," "curse," and "desiring"; some are images like "all alone," "beweep," and "trouble deaf heaven." Another effective feature is the sentence structure—the piling up of complaints in parallel clauses intensifies the tone of despair while adding the impression that the speaker is simply complaining too much. Yet another feature is the paradox in line 8, "With what I most enjoy contented least," which seems to emphasize the speaker's unreasonableness again.

Then, in line 9, comes the preparation for a change. "Yet . . ."; and with the first words of line 10, the tone changes markedly, rising rapidly to the climax in ". . . sings hymns at heaven's gate." From self-pity and despair, the tone has shifted quickly and dramatically to one of joy and happiness. The new tone is signalized by several things: by the word "haply," which ambiguously means "by chance" while it suggests "happily"; by the pause in the rhythm after "thee" to emphasize the source of the joy and to mark the moment of change; and by the familiar yet vividly presented simile of the "lark at break of day arising / From sullen earth"—as well as by other stylistic elements. Analyzing the tone of a poem like this one, which is primarily an expression of the writer's state of mind, can reveal the whole structure and fabric.

Tonal analysis will always reveal much that is important to the definition of a work's meaning and character. In many cases, a description of tone will amount to a description of the very style of a particular work, or will point to such a description: in Shakespeare's sonnet, for example, the identification of tone as "despairing" or "joyful" indicates that the style is personal and lyrical (that is, expressing emotion), and perhaps even expressionistic. It is fully as important to describe style accurately as it is tone, and now that we have considered most of the basic elements of style,

we are in a good position to do so, especially if we continually refer
to those specific elements—the kind of sentence structure, the nature of the allusions—as our means of definition, in addition to
applying the appropriate general adjectives. At the same time,
there are further subtleties and refinements of style which can
make our analysis more acute and precise.

SUBTLETIES AND REFINEMENTS

SPECIAL PROBLEMS OF STYLISTIC ELEMENTS

Diction, as we have defined it, is choice of words, short or
long, common or strange. And words may be invented as well as
chosen and new uses for words may be devised. Artificial devices
of diction like these are often very effective. Coined words, novel
compounds ("cinemactor"), and "portmanteau" words (for example, from Lewis Carroll's *Through the Looking Glass:* "slithy," from
"slimy" and "lithe") are to be found here and there; in parts of
James Joyce's *Ulysses* they are principal feature of the style, as in
the following description of organ music:

> But wait. But hear. Chordsdark. Lugugugubrious. Low. In a cave
> of the dark middle earth. Embedded ore. Lumpmusic.

Somewhat more common is the use of familiar words for new
purposes or functions. A number of inventive writers have changed
the grammatical functions of words, using nouns as verbs, for instance, and adverbs as adjectives; Shakespeare, in *Hamlet,* writes,
". . . all his visage wann'd [paled]" (Act II, scene 2), and in *Antony and Cleopatra,* he writes of the Egyptian queen, "Age cannot wither her nor custom stale [make stale] / Her infinite variety
. . ." (Act II, scene 2). And Keats, in stanza 27 of "The Eve of
St. Agnes," writes that "the warmth of sleep" "fatigued away"
Madeline's soul, which was thus "havened both from joy and

pain." Similarly, various writers—most recently and notably Dylan Thomas—have used words in new senses or new contexts; they have invented new meanings for old words, as it were, deriving the new from the old by association, almost metaphorically:

> Though wise men at their end know dark is right,
> Because their words had forked no lightning they
> Do not go gentle into that good night.
>> ("Do Not Go Gentle Into That Good Night")

> Now as I was young and easy under the apple boughs
> About the lilting house and happy as the grass was green . . . .
>> ("Fern Hill")

A second problem of diction, subtle yet often crucial, is that of the nature of the epithets. The problem as Herbert Read defined it in *English Prose Style:*[2] is multiple: Are the particular adjectives and adverbs necessary? Are they appropriate? Are they not simply appropriate but felicitous—notably apt?

Most good students have had it drummed into them, and many first-rate writers (Hemingway, for one) insist that the number of adjectives and adverbs employed should be sharply limited by necessity. As a matter of principle many writers try to use only those modifiers that are necessary to the reader's full comprehension of the work. This means, on the simplest level, that if the age, say, of a certain man crossing a street is important, then one should write something like, "the elderly man . . . ," or "the young man . . ."; but if his age is not important, these writers argue, it should not be mentioned. At the same time, different writers conceive of the "necessity" of modifiers in different ways, some arguing that an adjective may be necessary to the development of the tone or atmosphere though irrelevant otherwise. Writers who limit themselves to "necessary" adjectives and adverbs develop a more restrained, sparer style than that of writers who achieve fullness and color by means of modifiers over and above the minimum required.

[2] New York, 1952.

The other stages of the question about epithets involve value judgments; essentially, they ask first whether a given modifier is the proper one, the correct one for the context, and second whether it is not simply appropriate but especially memorable. We might ask, for instance, if the adjective "golden" in line 30 of Yeats's "Sailing to Byzantium" is appropriate, meditating such alternatives as "silver," "aureate," or—facetiously—"great big":

> Once out of nature I shall never take
> My bodily form from any natural thing,
> But such a form as Grecian goldsmiths make
> Of hammered gold and gold enameling
> To keep a drowsy Emperor awake;
> Or set upon a golden bough to sing
> To lords and ladies of Byzantium
> Of what is past, or passing, or to come.

In the context of this poem's plea for the enduring significance of spirit, art, and myth, "golden" is especially felicitous because of its associations with Sir James Frazer's famous study of ancient myths, *The Golden Bough,* among other things.

The third and last special problem of diction that we might consider now is that of "noun style" and "verb style." These are matters of sentence structure as well as diction; they involve the question of whether the key words, the most meaningful words, in a piece of writing are the nouns or the verbs. Some writers tend to depend heavily on nouns and their modifiers to carry the meaning, using verbs (mainly the verb "to be") merely as links between the nouns, while other writers employ more active and significant verbs, relying primarily on them. It is argued—with a good deal of justification—that a verb style has more vitality than a noun style, that the latter seems more static and passive. This different weight assigned to nouns and verbs helps determine the nature of the writer's style as a whole. In poetry, the effects of imagery, figurative language, sound, and rhythm modify verb and noun style a good deal, but in prose the difference is often very notable; brief quotations should make the general tendencies of the two styles clear:

> The Island of Capri was dark and damp on that evening. But for a while it grew animated and lit up, in spots, as always in the hour of the steamer's arrival. On the top of the hill, at the station of the *funiculaire,* there stood already the crowd of those whose duty it was to receive properly the Gentleman from San Francisco. The rest of the tourists hardly deserved any attention . . . .

> But here the stentorian voice of the second gong sounded throughout the house, as in a heathen temple. And having risen hurriedly, the Gentleman from San Francisco drew his tie more taut and firm around his collar, and pulled together his abdomen by means of a tight waistcoat, put on a dinner-coat, set to rights the cuffs, and for the last time examined himself in the mirror . . . .

Both of these passages, we should note, are from Ivan Bunin's short story "The Gentleman from San Francisco"; whether the style is "noun" or "verb" depends partly on a writer's general tendency and partly on the specific function or nature of particular passages in a single work.

Two other devices of style worth noting are clearly matters of sentence structure: first, the use of parallelism, balance, and antithesis; and second, the use of an inverted word order.

Parallel constructions are well recognized and widely used; all competent writers employ them for variety. When a writer habitually or commonly develops his sentences by means of parallel words, phrases, or clauses, his style is out of the ordinary; a style measurably characterized by parallelism has a tempo, a rhythm, and a flavor generally quite distinctive. This is particularly true if in addition, as is often the case, the parallel elements tend to be balanced; that is, logically complimentary or antithetical. The total effect is very much like that of Pope's heroic couplets: there is a neatness and grace, a symmetry, that has appealed to many writers, especially those of eighteenth century England, despite the fact that such a style can be stiff and artificial. This danger no doubt explains why this style is rarely used for straight narrative, but is more likely to be found in descriptive or explanatory passages.

In *Gulliver's Travels* we can find passages of parallelism and balance, particularly in the clauses beginning with "sometimes":

> The Emperor holds a stick in his hands, both ends parallel to the horizon, while the candidates advancing one by one, sometimes leap over the stick, sometimes creep under it backwards and forwards several times, according as the stick is advanced or depressed. Sometimes the Emperor holds one end of the stick, and his minister the other; sometimes the minister has it entirely to himself . . . .
>
> (Book I)

And we can find them easily, too, in much of Pope's poetry, as hinted above:

> True Wit is Nature to advantage dressed,
> What oft was thought, but ne'er so well expressed . . . .
> ("Essay on Criticism," ll. 297–298)

> Whether the nymph shall break Diana's law,
> Or some frail China jar receive a flaw;
> Or stain her honour or her new brocade . . . .
> ("Rape of the Lock," II, ll. 106–108)

In the first passage, "oft was thought" and "ne'er so well expressed" are parallel in grammatical structure and antithetically balanced in meaning. In the second passage, "whether" introduces parallel clauses, and then in the last line, the "or's" link balanced clauses.

The other device of sentence structure, inversion, depends for its effect on the fact that there is a "normal" word order for English sentences. Thus, most readers would expect to read "I gave him the book" or "I gave the book to him." If they encountered an inversion, "To him I gave the book," or "The book I to him gave," they might be startled or disconcerted and at the same time be struck by the force of the novel word order and the new emphasis it puts on one phrase or another of the sentence—"To him" or

"The book." Inversions such as these are often artificial or stiff, like neatly balanced constructions, and it is precisely because they are artificial that they can be so effective. Milton achieves striking effects in *Paradise Lost* through inversion, especially when he combines it with an involved sentence structure. Consider the first sentence of Milton's epic:

> Of man's first disobedience, and the fruit
> Of that forbidden tree, whose mortal taste
> Brought death into the world, and all our woe,
> With loss of Eden, till one greater Man
> Restore us, and regain the blissful seat,
> Sing, heavenly Muse . . . .

Milton here achieves an impressive dignity and elevation partly by means of inversion; elsewhere, he and other writers achieve various other effects. A famous instance has been cited already: "Irks care the crop-full bird? Frets doubt the maw-crammed beast?" (Robert Browning, "Rabbi Ben Ezra"); here the inversion helps to produce the cacophony. In stanzas 24 and 25 of "The Eve of St. Agnes," Keats achieves yet another effect, of the romantic and picturesque: "A casement high and triple-arched there was . . ." and "Full on this casement shone the wintry moon. . . ."

All of these devices and elements of style can produce a wide range of effects depending on how and where they are employed. This is especially true in the case of allusion, as we have already clearly seen from the variety of possible sources. Another important variation is in the manner of the allusion, whether made in passing or highly developed, whether covert or explicit, and whether incidental or crucial to the meaning or significance of the work or passage.

Let us consider again Milton's sonnet "On His Blindness":

> When I consider how my light is spent
>   Ere half my days in this dark world and wide,
>   And that one talent which is death to hide
>   Lodged with me useless, though my soul more bent
> To serve therewith my Maker, and present

> My true account, lest He returning chide,
> "Doth God exact day-labor, light denied?"
> I fondly ask. But Patience, to prevent
> That murmur, soon replies, "God doth not need
> Either man's work or His own gifts. Who best
> Bear His mild yoke, they serve Him best. His state
> Is kingly: thousands at His bidding speed,
> And post o'er land and ocean without rest;
> They also serve who only stand and wait."

In this, allusion is made to the parable of the talents (coins) in
Matthew 25:14–30. The allusion is crucial to the poem, because
of the analogy—and the contrast—between Milton's case and that
of the servant who was given one talent, an analogy that provides
not only the subject but also the theme of the poem. Yet Milton
does not refer specifically to the Bible, nor does he refer very explicitly to the story of a master's giving his servants some talents.
By virtue of the ambiguity of "talent," which refers to a poetic apti-
tude as well as to a coin, one can find the sense of the sonnet very
satisfactory without recognizing the allusion; the allusion is thus
covert (we can contrast it in this respect to the explicit reference to
Hamlet in Eliot's "Prufrock"). As these examples show, there is
little correlation between the importance, the centrality of the allusion, and the clarity with which it is made. In fact, it is hard to determine why some allusions are explicit while others are not: it is
probably a matter of the author's personal preference, and perhaps
of literary principles—or fashions.

With regard to the stylistic elements we called "special" (ambiguity, irony, and paradox) there is little to add now in the way of
general information or clarification. The nature of the effects of the
devices varies so greatly, and sometimes so subtly, from instance to
instance that it is best to move directly to observations and analyses of specific cases in order to clarify our conception of the devices.

Here another word of warning is in order: we often need to be
deliberately on the lookout for ambiguity and irony if we are to

perceive them, for they are covert by nature. This is not true in the case of verbal paradox, which is usually evident enough; it is only when the paradox resides in the relationship between characters, events, and places that it is likely to evade us. But ambiguity and irony, either verbal or situational, are inherently covert. Often we can see one possible meaning of an ambiguous expression but no other until it is pointed out to us—or until we have accustomed ourselves to the possiblity that other meanings exist. Similarly, we may take ironic statements at their face value unless we deliberately foster our consciousness of literary techniques. And this is almost doubly true in the case of situational irony or ambiguity, although those problems are outside the limits of our concern with style.

The foregoing should not suggest that ambiguity, irony, and paradox are nasty little tricks with words that an author will play on us if we don't watch out. On the contrary, they are symptoms or manifestations of one of the most basic functions of imaginative literature, that of correlating apparently fragmented and heterogeneous experience. One might say that most, if not all, literature is basically a confrontation of different kinds of experience, that it is based on the assumption that we can enjoy or profit from considering the relationships between things, situations, and concepts that we more ordinarily consider separately.

A writer's similes and metaphors are comparisons which draw together disparate things ("My love is like a red, red rose"). A tragedy shows us that good and evil, pity and justice are not totally inconsistent or mutually exclusive (King Lear is noble but irrational, and while we feel sorry for him, we feel that his end is deserved). Even a melodrama full of ghosts or a farce full of improbable coincidences is an enjoyable confrontation of our mundane existence with fantasy. When we consider imaginative literature in this light, we can see the fundamental significance of ambiguity, irony, and paradox. Ambiguity signifies different meanings for the same thing, paradox is the fusion of mutually contradictory elements, and irony results from the collocation of appearance and reality: all embody or depend on establishing a relationship between things normally considered separately. Manifested verbally, they present their ultimate significance explicitly.

GENERAL VARIETIES OF STYLE

We have been discussing many different elements and techniques, or different kinds of devices, that create the style of particular passages or of a writer's work in general. We have seen, for instance, that one style might be produced partly by an esoteric vocabulary and that another might result partly from long and rambling sentences. The question still before us is "What is the total effect of these elements working simultaneously?" or "What different kinds of style do all these devices and techniques produce when they interact?" Although there are many variables involved, we can perceive certain species of styles, certain general ways in which styles vary (much as we described varieties of rime schemes). Let us distinguish five different areas of variation: of level of usage, of personality, of amplitude, of degree of abstraction, and of emotionality.

The differences in level of usage, or "elevation," are those between the dignity and formality of *Paradise Lost,* the deft informality of *Gulliver's Travels,* and the colloquial or "familiar" style of a popular song. A formal style is characterized by long and often involved sentences, high-flown diction, and the like ("Let us partake of a repast"); a colloquial style, at the other extreme, generally pays little attention to strict grammar, and uses such things as slang ("Let's get a bite"); while an informal style lies between the extremes ("Let's get something to eat"). Styles may vary in level according to the type and function of the literary works and also according to the general tendency of the writers (Dickens' style is generally less formal than, say, Henry James's). The level of usage can also vary within a single work, according to the character speaking, or according to the function of particular passages—the level of *Paradise Lost* is not uniformly high, for instance; it is very dignified in the great invocations like the one at the beginning of the epic, which was quoted above, but it is fairly informal when the poet is describing Adam and Eve's domestic life before the Fall.

The degree of a style's elevation can perhaps be traced specifically to its kind of diction and its phrasing and sentence structure. The next variation in style, that in "personality," is the result of many stylistic elements. The total effect at one extreme is to make the reader continually conscious of the personality of the writer, or, conversely, to make the writer almost totally unobtrusive. At this point we run into an interesting problem. A first-rate writer is almost by definition one whose style is distinctive. We can recognize the Miltonic "organ voice" style, as well as the direct and simple style of Hemingway and the relaxed conversational style of Frost: these men's styles are their own, being clearly personal, even idiosyncratic. To say that Dryden and Hardy—and Shakespeare—do not have as personal a style seems to suggest that they are not the literary geniuses that the others are, though this is not true. It is reasonable to condemn a writer whose style is colorless and impersonal, but above a certain level there is a great deal of latitude in the extent to which a good writer's style may reflect his personality. And we should note that the literary genre may affect the personality of the style: in a play, the style has to be suited to the character rather than to the author.

Third, style may vary in amplitude. At the one extreme we find the rich and highly developed style of Spenser, Conrad, and Faulkner; at the other we find the spare, even laconic, style of Thomas Hardy, Emily Dickinson, and Hemingway. The following passages will illustrate:

> The narrow creek was like a ditch: tortuous, fabulously deep; filled with gloom under the thin strip of pure and shining blue of the heaven. Immense trees soared up, invisible behind the festooned

draperies of the creepers. Here and there, near the glistening black-
ness of the water, a twisted root of some tall tree showed amongst
the tracery of small ferns, black and dull, writhing and motionless,
like an arrested snake. The short words of the paddlers reverberated
loudly between the thick and somber walls of vegetation. Darkness
oozed out from between the trees, through the tangled maze of the
creepers, from behind the great fantastic and unstirring leaves; the
darkness, mysterious and invincible; the darkness scented and
poisonous of impenetrable forests.

(from "The Lagoon," by Joseph Conrad)

> The heart asks pleasure first;
> And then, excuse from pain;
> And then, those little anodynes
> That deaden suffering;
>
> And then, to go to sleep;
> And then, if it should be
> The will of its Inquisitor,
> The liberty to die.

(Emily Dickinson)

The one stylistic tendency seems to be to "surround" the subject or
topic, exploring it fully, presenting it in many different lights, in all
its complexity; the contrary tendency is to strike sharply and directly at the heart of the subject, to identify the essential elements
and present them immediately and without confusing distractions.

Next, style can also vary in degree of abstraction, that is, from
sensuousness to cold intellectuality, depending largely on such
things as the quantity and nature of the imagery and of the figures
of speech, and on the vitality of the verbs employed. Imaginative
literature, by its essential nature, will always be relatively sen-
suous, but the difference between the styles of Keats or Conrad on
the one hand and those of Pope and Henry James on the other
demonstrates that some writers have a keener sense or a fuller appreciation of the physical world than others.

Finally, the emotional intensity of style varies from author to
author, as well as from work to work and passage to passage. The

style in violent or sentimental episodes of Dickens' novels, for instance, obviously helps to heighten the emotional impact, while in more uneventful parts of the book the style is much more restrained. We can easily find other examples of such variation within a work; in fact, if a work of any length maintained the same emotional intensity throughout it would seem seriously defective. Particular authors, nevertheless, tend to write in a more highly "charged" style than others; those writers feel things more intensely, or express their feelings more readily. Let us contrast Shelley, say, with Frost in this respect:

> Hail to thee, blithe spirit—
> Bird thou never wert—
> That from heaven or near it
> Pourest thy full heart
> In profuse strains of unpremeditated art.
>
> (from "To a Skylark")

> Far in the pillared dark
> Thrush music went—
> Almost like a call to come in
> To the dark and lament.
>
> But no, I was out for stars:
> I would not come in.
> I meant not even if asked,
> And I hadn't been.
>
> (from "Come In")

We are ready now to consider literary style with adequate precision and comprehensiveness. We have identified the main elements of style—the ingredients that make it up—and we have noted the major kinds of "chemical compounds" or general styles that are formed by the interaction of the ingredients. For a full understanding and appreciation we must consider style on the two levels: on that of the action and the interaction of elements in restricted contexts, and on that of a work as a whole, especially in relation to the other aspects of the work.

6 ⚕⚕⚕⚕⚕⚕⚕⚕⚕⚕⚕

Tragedy

In this chapter we begin a consideration of concepts related to the "subjects" of literary works. We are going to concern ourselves, that is, with what the words are all about, what their point is, what they add up to. When we touch on material that concerned us in previous chapters we will consider it as part of a larger dimension. In defining tragedy, specifically, we must take into account the "objects" (character, action, setting) and the verbal tools (language, style) in works we call tragedies, but we will be primarily concerned with a broader aspect of literature, one which is perceived through those objects and tools. We will be generalizing and synthesizing on a higher level than before.

BASIC TERMS AND CONCEPTS

Most loosely a tragedy is a profoundly sad event or situation. In literature the term is conventionally reserved for a type of drama in which the protagonist is defeated, the material of the play being treated seriously and loftily. There is no need to restrict the literary meaning too narrowly, however; tragedy appears in the novel, the short story, and in poetry as well as in drama. The literary form, the genre, is not the essence of tragedy. This essence we must now investigate. Although different cultures and different ages have different ideas of what tragedy is, there are certain basic characteristics inherent in all those works usually considered tragic by perceptive readers.

THE TRAGIC HERO

To begin with, the protagonist in tragedy, called the tragic hero, has certain general characteristics: he is almost always fundamentally good, he is a capable person, and he is somehow humanly significant.

First, that is, he is almost never so evil in his principles or his behavior that he thoroughly deserves whatever bad end he comes to. We do not consider the destruction of evil tragic. If the hero's end is "tragic" he is the kind of person we are somewhat sad, not glad, to see defeated. He may not be purely good, but he is almost never purely bad; we find it hard to lament the destruction of a malevolent megalomaniac like Hitler, for instance, or of a cunning villain like Iago (who tricked Othello into killing his beloved wife out of jealousy, in Shakespeare's play). These get what they deserve, and the world is well rid of them.

Second, the tragic hero is capable to some extent of resisting effectively the persons or forces that oppose him. He is powerful enough, clever enough, or determined enough so that the conflict he is engaged in is not completely one-sided. The crushing of a helpless weakling may be sad—pitiful, that is—but it is not as important, as grave, as the defeat of a person we respect. Here lies the difference between tragedy and pathos: we would have felt sorry if Tiny Tim, the little crippled son of the poor clerk in Dickens' "Christmas Carol," had died—in fact the occasion might have been powerfully sentimental—but it would have been pathetic rather than tragic. Tiny Tim could do nothing to fight back; all he could do was suffer helplessly. Màcbeth, in contrast, fought continually and effectively in one way or another against the persons and forces that opposed him; even when he realized, at the end, that in Macduff he had met the only person who could kill him, he fought bravely and capably. The defeat of a person like that is impressive; it evokes more than pitying tears.

Third, the tragic hero is significant because he represents mankind in some way. He may stand for man simply by being characteristic—by embodying fundamental human traits—or he may represent man at his best or most eminent or as an ideal. Kings, princes, and noblemen were considered proper tragic heroes up through most of the eighteenth century because they clearly had considerable symbolic stature as human beings while the lower classes seemed not to. Nowadays, on the other hand, we are more inclined to maintain that, since social position is less significant than the intrinsic or acquired worth of the individual, any "true" man could be a tragic hero. Thus Arthur Miller's *Death of a Salesman* has been called a tragedy even though its protagonist is the salesman Willy Loman.

Taking the last two characteristics of the typical tragic hero together we can see that he has some kind of stature: he is a leader, at least potentially, for he is an effective person and at the same time embodies, symbolically, mankind in general. He is not too eccentric nor too ordinary, for he inspires sympathy and respect and makes us feel that he and what happens to him are important to us as human beings.

TRAGIC ACTION

These are the elemental qualities of a tragic hero; now to the basic nature of tragedy itself. What happens to the hero?

What happens is some kind of catastrophe, some devastating

defeat for the hero. This does not necessarily mean the protagonist's death. *Oedipus,* for instance, ends with the king's blinding
himself and his being exiled; for what he has done (killed his father,
had children by his own mother) death is perhaps too easy a way out.
Still, most tragic catastrophes involve the death of the hero, since
that is usually the most thorough defeat. The essential quality, nevertheless, is this defeat, not personal destruction; what counts is the
destruction of whatever is particularly important to the hero in the
context of the action. What is important may vary: it could be his
personal ambitions, political or social; it could be his belief in himself; it could be his whole set of values or his conception of the nature of things. Whatever it is, its importance is fundamental, and
when it is destroyed, the hero is clearly and substantially defeated.
He may in consequence be exiled, or die, or he may seem to go on
living almost conventionally; what happens as a result of his defeat, if the two steps are distinguishable, is not so important as the
defeat itself, although we often use the term "catastrophe" for the
hero's personal suffering. Thus, though we may call Macbeth's
death at Macduff's hands the catastrophe, the essential culmination
of the tragedy is the manifestation, in the fight with Macduff, of
the fact that Macbeth's ambitions and egotistical career are empty
and unstable.

The action in the plot also reveals another basic characteristic of
tragedy, that of causation, and therefore, of the action's particular
relevance to the protagonist. What happens to a tragic hero, in
other words, is clearly the consequence of what he has done or
what he is. A plot by definition is a causal series of events, but ac-
cidents and coincidences can play a part within that kind of framework; the degree of causality may be more or less obvious. The
plot of a tragedy, however, is clearly and emphatically causal. The
events move in a progression governed fundamentally and obviously by causation: the sequence of events is necessary, even inevitable, in the long run. This necessity is determined by a number of
different kinds of things: by the character of the hero, by the circumstances in which he finds himself, by the nature of society and

of mankind in general, or by fate in some sense or form. The outcome of the progression is due to qualities, circumstances, or forces peculiar to the particular hero; without this particularity the events could happen to anyone, as it were, and could thus seem due purely to chance. The essential point is that the tragic hero's catastrophe seems to us a logical consequence, and it seems such because the events that lead up to it do not occur haphazardly but because of their connection with the hero. Because the events in a tragedy are peculiarly relevant to him—even inescapable—they are logical.

Random accident, in other words, does not produce tragedy: the tragic hero is to some extent responsible for what happens to him, either because he is a certain kind of person, or because he is a member of a certain social group, or simply because he is part of mankind. Just as he is competent, and in fact because he is an effective person, he is in part responsible for his end. A defeat or destruction due to pure chance is sad, but we do not consider it tragic except in a very loose sense. The only way that chance may be truly tragic is for it to be a manifestation of social forces, say, or of fate, in some form relevant to the hero.

Let us consider a hypothetical case. Imagine a story about a man married to a wife he loves, with fine children, and securely established in a satisfying job. Supposing him to be a good and happy person, we would consider it sad for him to be killed suddenly in an automobile accident; we might even say, loosely, that his death was "tragic." But for this narrative to be more accurately called a tragedy, several elements are needed, among them the impression that the man's death was caused—by himself, or by external forces or circumstances that he was contending against. The story might be a tragedy, for example, if the accident were the result of some persistent psychological problem that the hero had been seriously struggling with, that is, if the accident were the result of a genuine problem in his life, not merely a random mischance. Or alternately the accident could be presented as a manifestation of the social forces enmeshing modern man; indirectly the hero would be responsible for his fate, sufficiently so for us to call it tragic, because as a man he helped to produce those forces (urbanization and mechanization, for example) and they are therefore relevant to him.

Finally, as we can see when we consider the preceding characteristics together, a tragedy is in a broad sense morally significant. The nature of the hero, his attitudes and behavior, and his fate are important not simply for their entertainment value or their esthetic worth but because they suggest some kind of moral theme. By *moral* we mean concerned with human evaluation of the good, the true, and the beautiful. Thus what happens to the tragic hero in particular reveals something important about what all men are or should be. This kind of thematic significance is found in a great deal of literature; indeed, a good many comic works embody a valid and important theme—that is, they have a serious point to them. On the other hand, many supposedly serious works lack this significance; melodrama, by definition, has little or no genuine moral point to it. The distinction between tragedy and melodrama is instructive: melodrama is entertainment on a fairly superficial level, providing sensational and emotional excitement primarily, while tragedy appeals to man's intellect and his spirit. Melodrama may be sensuously and esthetically satisfying, but it lacks tragedy's serious theme. Thus the westerns and other adventure serials we see on television can be serious but they are usually exciting without being thematically significant. On the other hand, though the ghost scene (not to mention the witches' scene) in *Macbeth* is sensational, even melodramatic when taken by itself, it is a vital part of a serious thematic fabric that helps make the play a genuine tragedy.

TRAGIC IRONY

A final basic concept connected with tragedy that we should discuss now is that of "tragic irony." In Chapter 5, on style, we considered verbal irony, the overt expression of a contrast between appearances and reality, as when we say the opposite of what we mean in order to intensify our meaning, by inversion. Tragic irony, too, is based on this contrast between what seems and what actually is. It is a form of situational or dramatic irony, the irony which emerges unexpressed from a situation or an action. Blessings disguised as misfortune, apparent strokes of luck that turn out to be curses—these involve dramatic irony. And the situation of the legendary Greek prophets—like Tiresias, in *Oedipux Rex*—who could foretell the future but whom no one would believe is equally dramatic irony. All these are ironic because what seems to be one thing is actually almost the opposite: the prophets' apparently marvelous gift is really worthless.

Such examples as these might suggest that irony resides in exceptional and peculiar circumstances, that it is a special device occasionally used by clever writers for unusual effects. That this is not the case, however, has already been pointed out in Chapter 5. Like ambiguity and paradox, irony is the result of looking at the world with mature and sophisticated eyes, with the realization that things are often not what they seem, or are considerably more than they seem on the surface. They are the result of the writer's mature vision, which considers experience not in single simple units but as a complex whole whose various parts and facets can enjoyably or profitably be considered in relation to each other. Indeed, the multiplicity which is the basis of irony is inherent in existence, in our experience: a child, though young and vigorous, is also ultimately on the road to death; a mixture of dried oils spread on a piece of canvas may at the same time be an object of great beauty; and the earth itself—in its seas and mountains, for example—is at the same time beautiful and terrible, beneficent and destructive.

Tragic irony, specifically, is dramatic irony which reinforces and intensifies a tragedy. For one reason or another it is inherent in tragedy, although it may or may not be emphasized in a particular work, because a tragedy is the story of a fundamentally admirable and competent hero who comes to grief. The resulting contrast between the basic nature of the hero on the one hand and the defeat that he suffers on the other is unavoidably ironic; he seems destined to success but is actually doomed to failure. More particularly, the hero inevitably acts rightly, does what he has to do, or feels that he is doing so, yet to no avail. Either the hero should take some other course of action, or there is nothing that can be done; in either case, tragic irony emerges from the contrast between what seems to be the right thing for the hero to do and what actually is so, between what might have been and what actually is. Thus Oedipus seems right to search for the murderer of the king that preceded him, but that very search will destroy him because without knowing it, he himself is the murderer. And it seems right to Macbeth to pursue the destiny revealed by the witches, and necessary to kill those who stand in his way, yet the more he does to achieve his destiny and the more he fulfills it, the more worthless and insecure it becomes.

SUBTLETIES AND REFINEMENTS

Many historical, critical, and philosophical problems are involved in the definition and analysis of tragedy, especially when we go beyond the basic elements. We must aim at a clear conception of the variety and the dimensions of the subtleties and refinements of the subject.

GENERAL CHARACTERISTICS OF TRAGEDY

There are, to begin with, a number of other characteristics of tragedy which have often been noted. These are not fundamental or invariable enough to be dealt with as basic concepts, but they must be considered now if our conception of tragedy is to be valid.

First let us look again at the nature of the tragic hero. We have seen that he is almost never completely evil, that he is capable, and that he has considerable stature as a leader or a symbol of mankind. Now more specifically we can observe that he is one of at least three types of persons. Most commonly—thanks to Aristotle's description of the Greek tragic hero—he is defined as a good man whose character nevertheless contains a serious flaw (Aristotle's term *hamartia* is often used) that is connected directly or indirectly with his downfall. Macbeth has been considered an example of this type, his flaw being his ambition; and Hamlet, with his "fatal indecision," has been cited, too. The most common, and indeed the typical, fatal flaw among the Greek tragic heroes—and later ones as well—is pride, or a kind of overweening self-confidence (the Greek term *hubris* is often used). Oedipus demonstrates *hubris;* so does King Lear, in Shakespeare's play, with his insistence on having his daughters prove that they love him and on being treated like a monarch even after he has given his kingdom away.

A second type of tragic hero, such as Socrates, found in Plato's *Apology,* is the person who is completely flawless, or practically so, and who is not responsible for his defeat in the sense that he must be punished for his own mistake or misdeed, but brings destruction upon himself simply because of what he is, in the world as it is. Plato's narrative of the death of Socrates demonstrates the defeat of an almost thoroughly good hero by an evil society. One real danger in this kind of tragedy is that the hero may become merely an object of pity; since by objective standards he does not deserve his fate we may simply feel sorry for him, letting our pity overshadow any respect we may have for him. What prevents the narratives like the death of Socrates from being merely pathetic rather than tragic is partly the great stature of the protagonists. One cannot merely feel pity for them, because they are more than simply good; they are so noble and so capable that their destruction, and the token defeat of the good that it represents, is a supremely significant event.

Third, one occasionally finds exceptions to the observation that tragic heroes are never thoroughly bad: there are some evil heroes.

When tragedies of sinister protagonists are genuine tragedies, not simply object lessons about what happens to evil men, the stature of the hero is again a crucial factor. If a petty thief is caught and punished, we are not especially impressed. A truly great villain, on the other hand, an evil genius who suggests by his vision, his power, and his competence that he would have been a wonderful person had he not gone wrong, is genuinely admirable, from a certain distance. This type of hero is found in Christopher Marlowe's *Tamburlaine,* Part 2, an English play of the sixteenth century about a man who by treachery and brute force had transformed himself from a shepherd to a king of Persia, and then by pursuing his tyranny beyond all conceivable limits caused his own downfall. Tamburlaine's fall is tragic not because something basically good has been defeated but because something we admire, strength of character, has gone wrong and by doing so has destroyed itself. This kind of tragedy, certain critics argue, is less tragic than others; because the hero is not partly good he cannot "properly" be a tragic hero. Yet Macbeth, in one of Shakespeare's best-known tragedies, is this kind of hero. Tragedies of evil heroes are unusual, and are different from other kinds, but they are no less valid.

The other general, though variable, characteristic of tragedy that we should examine now is the nature of the conclusion as it affects the theme. It is generally agreed, as we have seen, that a tragedy by its very nature has some kind of thematic significance; despite the sorrow there is a positive element in the conclusion of a tragedy. This positive element may develop in at least three different ways, the difference being important to the whole effect of the work.

First and most commonly, the moral significance is actually achieved by the conclusion of the narrative; that is, the defeat of the hero is itself necessary to the development of the theme. One way (the most "respectable" way according to many moralists) for this theme to emerge is as a simple moral point, thus: a man who makes a serious mistake which has bad consequences, or who is responsible for serious misdeeds, is punished. This case can easily be made to sound rather simpleminded, but it is not necessarily so; moreover, if it is not the governing element in tragedy, it is certainly a common one. Thus Macbeth is punished for his misdeeds, Hamlet suffers partly because of his mistake of failing to act or for expecting too much of the world, and Faustus, who makes a pact with the Devil in Christopher Marlowe's *Doctor Faustus,* is punished by being dragged down to Hell at the end of his twenty-four years of ill-gotten worldly revelry.

Another way for the theme to be achieved by the conclusion is as a "victory in defeat." When the hero is clearly good and capable, it often happens that despite his defeat he attains something of significant value which partly offsets his defeat. Hamlet can again be cited, for he does succeed in punishing his father's murderer even though he himself is killed. The case is similar in several narrative poems by Robert Browning, such as "Childe Roland to the Dark Tower Came"; in this poem a knight on a quest for a mysterious Dark Tower achieves his goal although at that same moment he is destroyed by evil forces. This type of conclusion, too, can be simpleminded, but it can also be powerfully ironic: the plus and the minus elements, instead of canceling out, seem to reinforce each other, thereby intensifying the effect of the work as a whole.

A third way that a positive element is achieved at the conclusion of a tragedy is by an improvement in the hero himself. He may achieve a new maturity, or be regenerated in some fashion, or he may attain new insight into his own nature, into the motives or the psychological and moral significance of his actions and their consequences. The conclusion of the tragedy is catastrophic, that is, but at the same time it has important beneficial effects on the protagonist. Once again we can recall Hamlet, who attains a resolution and a calmness of mind that reveals a new maturity of character at the end of his life. Two of the clearest and most powerful examples of this type of conclusion are *Oedipus* and *King Lear.* In the first, the tragedy and the positive element both reside in the king's coming to see what he has done and what he is. In Shakespeare's play we see at the end that the once arrogant and foolish monarch attains a new humanity through the humility and wisdom he has learned from his errors and their consequences. Having exiled his loving daughter Cordelia and divided his kingdom between his two evil daughters, he is then ungratefully rejected by both in turn despite the efforts of friends and subjects who remain loyal, suffering sometimes cruelly on his behalf. When the evil daughters Goneril and Regan are finally defeated, and Cordelia is dead, Lear dies a nobler, though more sorrowful, king than he had ever been before.

These tragic endings function as the thematic culminations of the works; without them the works would be morally incomplete in the sense that they would lack the positive element which many critics consider a necessary part of a tragedy. There are other tragedies, however, in which the positive element consists of the persistence of values originally present in the work from the beginning. Although nothing positive is newly achieved at the end, the catastrophe is not thoroughly destructive, for an inherent moral good survives. Such a tragedy is Milton's epic poem *Paradise Lost;* Adam destroys his "original glory" (in Northrop Frye's words[1]) by disobeying God, and ends up not Man but merely the first man, with little, immediately, to look forward to. What he does have to look forward to, Christ's redemption of the human race and the defeat of Satan, is the carrying forward of the original vision that animated the action. The positive element in this work, in other words, is not achieved at the conclusion, but persists in its despite. The original vision of the universe and of Man in Eden is so great that it cannot be completely eradicated even though it seems in effect defeated. The case is similar in some of those works whose heroes are flawless: at the end of Plato's *Apology* the greatness of Socrates' character and achievements persists despite his execution.

[1] *Anatomy of Criticism,* Princeton, 1957, p. 212.

The variable characteristics of tragedy discussed above should make clear that there is no precise and immutable form of tragedy that we can isolate. What we can identify are the essential general elements and certain typical, though variable, characteristics. At various times, however, tragedy has been defined much more narrowly. The Greek conception differs from that of the Renaissance, as that does from the modern. We need to consider the various conceptions of tragedy, which lie behind the actual plays of the various periods, in order to understand the differences between the plays themselves. We will also come to realize more clearly thereby that our inclusive description of typical tragedy is the only serviceable kind of definition possible, and that there is no one "proper" variety of tragedy to the exclusion of all others.

First, the conception of the hero has varied considerably in accordance with cultural and critical variations, as we have noted above. Up through the eighteenth century it was generally assumed that he had to be of noble if not royal blood, while in recent times the idea that the hero could be a commoner has been widely accepted. The original assumption was due fundamentally to the further assumption that only the aristocracy had the necessary inherent eminence, and at the same time it was due to the establishment of that tradition during the first development of tragedy by the Greeks. In England during Shakespeare's time a few "domestic tragedies" were produced, in which the action involved common people and ordinary households. Similar material formed the basis for a number of sad, if not powerfully tragic, plays in the eighteenth century, but the full development of domestic tragedy (though the term is rarely used for our dramas) has come in the period of "modern drama," beginning in the middle of the nineteenth century with the Norwegian playwright Henrik Ibsen (see *Ghosts* or *Hedda Gabler,* for example). It is still argued that a genuine tragic hero must be out of the ordinary, a leader clearly "superior in degree to other men"[2] but, as various critics have pointed out, in a democratic age a commoner is considered acceptable as a hero.

In addition to differences in the conception of the tragic hero, there have been differences in the conception of the normal form and structure of the genre. To begin with, while tragedy has almost always been considered a form of drama, we have recently become accustomed to use the term for novels, short stories, and poems, not to mention motion pictures, when the nature and treatment of the material warrant it. We have come to feel that the essence of tragedy lies less in the form than in intrinsic—though general—characteristics.

Secondly, the conception of the structure of tragic drama has varied. This structure was for a long time conceived of as the fall of the hero from eminence to baseness or destruction, as Oedipus falls from a king "whom all men call the great" to a blind and despised outcast. In the English Renaissance this pattern can be seen in many plays: *Doctor Faustus, King Lear,* and *Othello,* for example. At the same time, another kind of structure was in evidence, that of the rise and then the fall. Thus Macbeth achieves greatness but then loses it, and Marlowe's Tamburlaine follows the same course in a pair of plays. This difference in structure is linked with another somewhat more general one, that between the drama of crisis and the "panoramic drama." Greek and Roman dramas and their direct descendants focused sharply on the critical point in the whole history of the hero; the action of the plays began shortly before the major climax (the crisis) and ended shortly thereafter. The "unities" (conventions, not requirements, it should be noted) emerged from this kind of structure: the action tended to be limited to a single clear line of development, the time-span to a single day, and the setting to a single place. In England this tradition was modified by the native tradition of "miracle plays," medieval dra-

[2] Frye, pp. 33–34.

matic productions that sometimes covered the whole history of the world from the creation to Doomsday. The result was the panoramic drama exemplified by Shakespeare's plays about various periods in English history, and by his *Antony and Cleopatra,* which covers several years and switches from Rome to Egypt and back several times. And of course *Macbeth* is panoramic drama, too. It is interesting to note, nevertheless, that in our time the panoramic drama has been taken over largely by the movies while the legitimate theater, restricted by various factors, has staged dramas of crisis for the most part. The importance of the differences in structure, finally, is that with the first type, the crisis drama of a fall, intensity is achieved by concentration, by focusing sharply and continuously on the most important part of the hero's story; the second type of tragic drama may be equally powerful, but its power is achieved partly by accumulation, that is, by the piling up of incident upon incident, and at least partly by emphasizing breadth and fullness in the treatment of the material rather than sharpness and intensity.

The last important variation in the conception of tragedy to recognize now is that concerning the cause of the hero's defeat, particularly in regard to the hero's responsibility for it. We touched on this problem briefly when we observed that the action in a tragedy is not accidental but logical, even inevitable, and that the hero is partly responsible for his fate, directly or indirectly. It is here that the problem arises: how directly is the hero responsible? In Greek tragedy it is apparent that the personal responsibility is often minimal, that is not so much what the hero *does* that causes his downfall as what he *is*. He may suffer because he is a member of a family that has incurred the enmity of a god, or because he is caught in a tragic dilemma which would destroy any man. The cause of the hero's defeat in these cases and similar later ones is usually identified as fate. In other words, the hero is beaten, as anyone would be, by forces beyond his control. These forces may take different forms: they may be the gods, they may be simply a combination of unlucky circumstances, they may be the laws or some other pressures of society. The hero may be good, bad, or good though flawed (if this last, the hero's flaw may merely help reconcile us to his suffering); in any case he is relatively helpless though he may seem very much the effective leader. Now although the fatalistic concept of tragedy is very old, and still common, there developed during the Renaissance (that is, during the fourteenth, fifteenth, and sixteenth centuries in Europe) a tendency to root the hero's defeat in his own character, to emphasize the flaw in that character and make it the cause of his downfall. Thus although Oedipus was doomed at birth by the curse of a god to commit horrible sins, and tried to avoid them in vain, Macbeth's crimes, and his ultimate destruction, are due to his ungovernable ambition. At present both concepts of the nature of the defeat are to be observed in operation, although on the one hand the hero's flaw may be completely subconscious, and on the other fate may take the form of the Existentialists' philosophical "absurdity" of life.

All these variations have often been considered either–or propositions, but without logical warrant, for they have all produced viable tragedies. Critics and writers have argued in the past, and indeed still do argue, that real tragedy is a conflict between man and fate, say, and never man against his own weakness or defects; or they have argued the opposite. Reverence for the brilliance of Aristotle's critical comments on Greek drama has led scholars and teachers to feel that he defined once and for all the veritable essence of tragedy, that anything else was not really tragedy—or else that it had to be forced somehow to agree with Aristotle's description. Undoubtedly there is reason to try to determine whether tragedy has essential characteristics, and if so, what they are, but we should not limit ourselves or oversimplify the argument by reducing it to a series of simple alternatives.

To conclude our discussion of tragedy we should now widen our perspective. We should recognize that tragedy can be considered from several different perspectives, each contributing something to our understanding of it. So far we have been dealing with it structurally, primarily identifying the intrinsic characteristics of the plot, the characters, and the setting. Now we should touch specifically on the relationship tragedy has with the audience and with society and human experience in general.

The effect of tragedy on the audience has been considered so important that it has often been cited as an identifying characteristic. According to Aristole tragedy has a powerful and a specific emotional effect on the audience, "through pity and fear effecting a proper purgation (*catharsis*) of these emotions." Either we get rid of pity (for the hero) and fear (of the forces causing his defeat) by having them aroused by tragedy, or these emotions of ours are cleansed by being aroused by the performance. Whichever is the case, Aristotle put his finger on the fact that our emotions, specifically those of pity and fear, are profoundly affected by tragedy in a particular way. The term *catharsis* is generally used with the understanding that the experience it stands for is a real and significant experience even if it cannot be precisely understood. We should note, however, that the concept of catharsis is only one formulation of tragedy's relationship with the audience; it has also been suggested that in tragedy we assist at a kind of reenactment of the ritual sacrifice of a hero or leader, that we are involved indirectly with the same kind of experience as that of ancient times in which the leader was sacrificed, symbolically perhaps, for the sake of the community. If this is the case, the psychological effect might be largely subconscious, but it would be profound and powerful.

Other studies of tragedy have related it significantly to general thematic and narrative patterns found throughout the literature of our Western culture. Various scholars and critics have described tragedy in terms of "modes" (general conceptions of man and experience) and in relation to myths (general patterns of action). Taking a cue from Aristotle yet again in his *Anatomy of Criticism,* Northrop Frye suggests that various governing frames of mind can be identified in literary works according to the relative positions of the protagonists and the audience, that is, according to whether the protagonist is superior, equal, or inferior to us. *Macbeth,* as a conventional tragedy, belongs to the mode characterized by a protagonist who is superior to us in degree (not in kind) though not to his and our environment, while *Death of a Salesman* is a less traditional tragedy because its protagonist is more nearly on our own level or even below it. In the same work Frye also examines literature from a "mythic" standpoint. Like other recent scholars and critics, he wishes to analyze literature according to the archetypal characters and actions represented; practically all literary works, it is argued, can be seen as variations or combinations of certain persistent kinds of characters and events. To be specific, tragedy typically embodies the general archetypal experience of the exclusion of an individual—that is, an extraordinary person, or one who doesn't "belong"—from society.[3] This archetypal pattern is evident in otherwise very different tragedies. *Oedipus Rex* and *Hamlet* clearly evidence the pattern, and Willy Loman, too, fails to belong to his society no matter how much he wants to. The modal and archetypal critical approaches attempt to synthesize the instrinsic characteristics of literature on a broad, inclusive foundation; they are turning out to be one of the most promising avenues of critical analysis of our time.

Looking beyond the borders of literary criticism we can see that tragedy can also be regarded as a general outlook on life, as suggested by the saying "Life is a comedy to those who think, a tragedy to those who feel." This outlook is implicit in literary works, for literature is certainly connected with the rest of human life

[3] Frye, p. 35.

rather than being separate and isolated. To be sure, we run the danger of oversimplifying this concept, for literature has its own identity, its own integrity. Yet in literature as elsewhere we find the elements of the tragic view of life: a concern with man's weakness and greatness in the face of the profound difficulties inherent in his existence, and with the complexity of man's moral problems. These concerns are reflected in all of the characteristics of tragedy and the tragic hero which we discussed in the first part of this chapter; the generality of those characteristics suggests that one way to determine the essence of tragedy is to analyze the literary works philosophically, in relation to the tragic view of life.

OTHER SERIOUS NARRATIVE

Tragedy, it should be clear by now, is not simply a kind of play in which the hero dies at the end; it is much more complicated as well as bigger and more important. It is one of the poles of human existence and of literature, the opposite pole being comedy. These poles are not separate; between them lies an array of works which are more or less tragic, more or less comic. Before we undertake a discussion of comedy (in Chapter 7) we must consider those kinds of narratives that fall between the poles; these are not thoroughly tragic, but they are serious.

Pathos, for one, is considered less important than tragedy because it is founded almost exclusively on pity for the protagonist. This pity is aroused when the protagonist is helpless to combat the forces or persons opposing him, while the tragic hero is capable and effective. The pathetic protagonist may be thoroughly likeable, even morally admirable, but if he is too weak or gentle to be impressive, to have any stature, then his defeat, though sad, is not fearful enough to be tragic. The fate of the Duchess in Browning's poem "My Last Duchess" is pathetic rather than tragic because she was too sweet and innocent to have a heroic stature, and too helpless against the Duke.

Another less than tragic genre that we have touched on is melo-drama, that kind of serious narrative which falls short of tragedy because it lacks thematic significance. Such a work may involve characters of considerable stature and competence, but if the de-feat of the hero is not really very important from a broadly moral point of view, if the work depends heavily on suspense and sur-prise in order to emphasize the action and the plot themselves rather than what they signify, we call it melodrama. The typical television western often falls into this category, as we have noted.

In the drama specifically there are recognized types of play that belong here. The "problem play" and what has been called the *"drame"* (pronounced *drahm*), in particular, should be identified. The *drame* is familiar enough to be easily recognizable: it is a play (or by extension any narrative) which is serious, and often solemn and lacrymose, through most of the action, but which ends happi-ly. It is a work that is generally tragic in tone but that ends not in a catastrophe but a fortunate resolution. Soap operas (when and if they ever end), as well as so-called women's movies and novels, are often *drames*. Plays of this kind are called "sentimental drama," too, for they stimulate emotion for its own sake, and beyond the degree reasonably warranted by the subject that produces the emo-tion (a person who enjoys tender tears stimulated by a picture of unhappy kittens is obviously sentimental).

The "problem play" and the "problem" novel or short story belong to a more respectable genre. These are the works which, as the name suggests, are concerned with some serious general prob-lem (if the problem is attached to a particular character, his is a representative case), usually social, but sometimes partly psycho-logical or philosophical. Such works may be tragedies as well, but even when the endings are not catastrophic, the works are genuine-ly serious and often profound. Many of Dickens' novels, though partly sentimental in genre, are "problem" novels; most of Hardy's novels are of this type, too, although many are also tragedies.

There are other kinds of works that fall between the tragic and the comic poles. Science fiction and other stories of "wonderful" adventure, for instance, and works that project into a narrative form the psychological experiences of the author certainly belong somewhere between the poles. This is also the case with satire; works like Swift's *Gulliver's Travels* are neither quite tragic nor quite comic in viewpoint or tone, yet have something of both in them. On the whole, however, these satires are fundamentally comic, since they are based on, and often aimed directly at, inconsistencies and incongruities in man and his behavior. We shall therefore discuss satire in the next chapter.

Comedy

Comedy, as it is conventionally conceived, is more generalized than tragedy: we treat almost all "entertaining" narratives as comedies of some kind, while we do not consider all "sad" stories tragic. We make distinctions between tragedy and melodrama, *drame,* the problem play and the pathetic play, but comedy is a comprehensive genre. Within it we distinguish between different types, some of which vary greatly on the surface from other members of the species. Despite this superficial variation, however, common denominators of comedy have been identified—characteristics that all comedies share no matter how they differ in details. Let us begin, then, with the basic concepts that apply to comedy in all its forms.

BASIC TERMS AND CONCEPTS

COMEDY AND THE AUDIENCE

Let us first consider the relationship between comedy and its audience. The general relationship is more definite and consistent than in the case of tragedy, and will reveal some crucial features of the genre.

First and most obviously, comedy is fundamentally entertaining. It may be informative or instructive in addition, but if it is not entertaining it is not comedy. By this we mean not simply that it is amusing, but that it has an element of "play," that we do not take it too seriously, and that it doesn't "matter" too much. Whereas tragedy bothers us because it deals seriously with significant moral issues, comedy does not affect us as much. It amuses us; it interests us for the moment, but when we are finished with it we are inclined to forget it.

Now this play element is connected closely with another commonly recognized characteristic of comedy, the fact that there is a considerable distance between it and its audience. By "distance" we mean what is called "esthetic distance," the degree of dispassionateness with which the audience regards the persons and events in a work of art. In comedy we are not greatly concerned for the persons in the story. We follow what happens to them as if we were looking down from a height, or as if they were not the same kind of people as we. If we, as audience, are psychologically involved in a narrative—if, for instance, we identify ourselves with the hero, participating in his adventures and emotions vicariously —the "distance" is small, while if we feel little immediate concern for the characters this distance is greater. Because the characters and events in comedy are not connected with us, what they do and are does not matter greatly; and because comedy has features that make it primarily entertaining, it does not require us to take it seriously. These first two characteristics of the relation between comedy and the audience, in other words, are interlocked.

One particular reason for the comic "distance" is crucial: the characters in a comedy are below the level of the audience, psychologically, if not socially. In tragedy the protagonist tends to be greater than we are, a leader or a man out of the ordinary. In comedy, on the other hand, the protagonist and the rest of the characters as well seem below us, as suggested when we noted that we look down on them as if from a height. If we are to laugh at comic characters they must be in some sense below us or at least no more than our equals. If we should "look up" to them—that is, respect and admire them—we should be unlikely to regard them as laughable. In the stock comic situation of a dignified gentleman slipping on a banana peel, we are amused by him precisely because he is brought low.

To illustrate the relation between comedy and its audience concretely, let us consider a perennial favorite, Oscar Wilde's *Importance of Being Earnest*. First of all, we do not take the happenings seriously; we know that even though Jack apparently becomes furious with Algy the fury is shallow and temporary, and we know, too, that even when it looks as if Gwendolyn will never be able to marry Jack (first because his name is not Earnest, and then because he was a foundling) some way will be found to overcome these obstacles—neither of which is especially serious in our eyes, anyway. Second, the distance between these events and us is great. The characters are in this case too unreal to be taken seriously: their behavior is irrational and artificial, and their speech too witty to be true. They have enough failings to make them human, like us, but they seem to accept these failings as normal, rational behavior, or as positive virtues (as when Algy invents a sick friend, Bunbury, in the country, in order to have an excuse to escape from the tedium of city life now and then). Finally, we can hardly consider these people our equals, despite their wit and their supposed high social position: they are not trying to be witty, but sensible, and their social position is belied by silly behavior (as when Cecily spitefully loads Gwendolyn's tea with sugar). These evidences of the particular relationship between the audience and comedy are to be found, to a greater or a lesser degree, in all comic works.

INTRINSIC CHARACTERISTICS OF COMEDY

The relationship of comedy to its audience that is discussed above reflects certain characteristics inherent in the fabric of comedy, features of the subject matter itself. The effect on the audience is clear evidence of the nature of comedy since we ourselves can serve as witnesses. At the same time, we must pay particular attention to the intrinsic characteristics, for these take us into the works themselves, independently of time and occasion.

Most essentially comedy emphasizes society rather than the individual. Tragedy is focused on the plight of the single hero, treating his greatness and his sufferings as more significant than the regular and normal behavior of the society he belongs to. Comedy, on the other hand, emphasizes just this regular and normal behavior. Typically, it deals with less exceptional cases of human action and motivation and it implies clearly, when it depicts this behavior, that it is to be looked down on because it runs counter to accepted standards. The general viewpoint in comedy is that of society as a whole, not that of the individual protagonist. This is the reason why admirable protagonists with whom we can identify ourselves are rare in comedy: if they are really eminent, they tend to counteract the social tendencies of the genre and thus change it into something a little different, and if we identify ourselves with them we cannot very easily laugh at them. Thus if the gentleman who slips and falls on the banana peel turns out to have been Abraham Lincoln, the episode is not really so funny after all; and the comedy of a "sad" clown like Charlie Chaplin is mixed with pathos because we put ourselves in his shoes, recognizing that his well-meant bumbling is like our own.

This emphasis on society is manifested in many ways. Behind them all lies the fact that comedy never concerns itself with really exceptional circumstances or behavior; the eccentric or whimsical actions of the characters, and the peculiar events that involve them, are never so far from the normal as to become "abnormal" or monstrous, or to deny the preeminence of society. The dignified gentleman may slip on a banana peel, but he does not fall off a cliff; or if he does fall off a cliff, he does not hurt himself any more seriously than he does when he slips on the banana peel, for such suffering would be "abnormal" enough to threaten the stability and comfort of our world.

Still further beneath the relationship with the audience lie the psychological foundations of comedy—what makes the comic characters funny. There is general agreement about the following. First, comedy derives from deviations from the norm, as long as they are not too great: a dog smoking a pipe, a love-sick miser, a henpecked husband who imagines himself as the brave captain of a storm-tossed ship. Especially, we find deviations from the social norm, or what most of us believe is the normal or the standard way for people to behave: the young man from the upper classes who turns out to have been found as a baby in a suitcase is such a deviation, as is our dignified gentleman who slips on the banana peel. It is worth noting, too, that many of these cases degrade the subject somewhat; many critics argue that this degradation is an important element in comedy. More generally, however, it is felt that the inconsistency or incongruity manifested in the deviations is the essential element; a chimpanzee who is bright enough to play checkers, or a supposedly poor and ignorant Indian who turns out to own oil wells worth millions, are comical even though they are elevated rather than degraded.

To be sure, not all inconsistency is comic; mild deviations from the norm can be treated as neutral facts. For comedy we need the elements touched on above, and in addition, the wit and humor with which they are imbued. These two ingredients of the comic mood are fundamental to the production of amusement; they are distinguished as follows. Humor is warmer, more emotional, perhaps more "human" than wit; wit is more intellectual, more subtle, and somewhat more artificial than humor. Because of these respective natures, wit is generally verbal, while humor is usually the result of concrete situations and actions. Such a story as James Thurber's "Secret Life of Walter Mitty" is humorous rather than witty: poor henpecked Mitty keeps being rudely awakened from his daydreams of heroism by rather discomfiting experiences, as when he imagines he commands a great seaplane flying through a storm only to be brought up short by his wife's telling him he's driving too fast. The amusement in this case is humor: it is colored by our sympathy for Mitty, and a feeling that this is just the kind of thing that happens to all of us. In *The Importance of Being Earnest,* on the other hand, much of the amusement comes from the wit of the dialogue, from the deft and paradoxical language. One short passage, for instance, goes like this:

> *Jack:* . . . If I marry a charming girl like Gwendolyn, and she is the only girl I ever saw in my life that I would marry, I certainly won't want to know Bunbury.
>
> *Algernon:* Then your wife will. You don't seem to realize, that in married life three is company and two is none.
>
> *Jack* (sententiously): That, my dear friend, is the theory that the corrupt French Drama has been propounding for the last fifty years.
>
> *Algernon:* Yes; and that the happy English home has proved in half the time.
>
> *Jack:* For heaven's sake, don't try to be cynical. It's perfectly easy to be cynical.
>
> *Algernon:* My dear fellow, it isn't easy to be anything now-a-days. There's such a lot of beastly competition about.

VARIETIES OF COMEDY

To complete our basic consideration of comedy, we need to identify the most important of the various kinds, distinguishing the principal types that have long and generally been recognized and that differ from each other in significant ways.

First, let us notice the distinction between "high" and "low" comedy. Of the two, low comedy is the more primitive and the more obviously comic; it constitutes that end of the scale where farce and slapstick are to be found. Here the humor is broad and obvious, usually based on physical situations and actions (farce, to be precise, is that kind of comedy whose humor depends on broadly improbable or incongruous situations and the like. Slapstick is a kind of farce that relies specifically on humorous action, like pie throwing). The amusement is emotional, and it is rarely colored by any attempt at a meaning or theme. Low comedy, characteristically, is pure and unsubtle humorous entertainment, though even so, there are considerable differences in quality between farces, as we can see from comparing the Three Stooges with the Marx Brothers.

At the "high" end of the scale we find literary comedies like Shakespeare's *Twelfth Night* and *As You Like It,* Bernard Shaw's *Caesar and Cleopatra* and *Pygmalion* (the basis for *My Fair Lady*), and the motion pictures which we can perhaps characterize by appropriate actors, such as Charles Boyer, Claudette Colbert, and Rex Harrison. In these comedies there is often no exuberant laughter, merely smiles and quiet chuckling. We are amused at times, but not violently; indeed some high comedies cannot really be called "funny" although nothing really sad happens in them and their general tone is pleasant and cheerful. Most are varied in tone, however, and they sometimes contain relatively low comic scenes like the one in *Caesar and Cleopatra* in which Cleopatra is carried off to see the Roman emperor, rolled up in a rug. On the whole, nevertheless, high comedy is witty rather than humorous, romantic rather than realistic (see Chapter 9); it is more serious than low comedy, fundamentally, for it usually has some point to it. We are entertained both by the actual events and characters, and also by the light shed on them, the perspective from which they are seen; even when this light or perspective does not constitute a specific theme, it can suggest a general attitude toward life and human experience. When it does so emphatically, and especially when this "meaning" is so developed that it becomes thematic, the comedy becomes something other than simple entertainment. It is to this offshoot of comedy that we turn now.

If we imagine a line between pure entertainment at one extreme and pure instruction at the other, we would have to place comedy close to the "entertainment" end, but at the same time we would surely realize that some comedy belongs further along the line toward the other end. The point at which comedy becomes significantly or largely instructive cannot be localized, but we know that in the kind of writing we call satire we are somewhere in the middle between the two extremes, partaking of both. To define the concept generally, satire is writing which more or less playfully attacks the vices and the follies of mankind. Whether or not it is able, or expected, to correct these defects, it at least brings them to our attention by making fun of them gently, moderately, or severely. That satire varies in intensity is evident from the difference between the gentle ribbing that absent-minded professors get on television and in the movies, and the "savage indignation" of Swift's "Modest Proposal" (mentioned in Chapter 5), in which he suggests that the only reasonable and practical way of solving the economic and social problems of the Irish is to sell their children to the English for food. Since satire has such a wide scope, varying as much as it does and functioning often so largely as instruction, it is often treated as a genre separate from comedy. Nevertheless, it does, by definition, entertain and indeed amuse us, though sometimes rather grimly. Its function is essentially to make us laugh at its subjects; when it loses that function, it becomes a direct attack, an argument (though such attacks may sometimes loosely be called satirical if they are pursued indirectly or especially dramatically). Satire, thus, is a variety of comedy that leads toward, but falls slightly short of, pure persuasion.

In addition to the varying degrees of intensity in satire that we have noted, there are variations in technique. The three most commonly identified ones are parody, caricature, and burlesque. All three are normally in the middle range of satire in intensity, though they are sometimes farcical and occasionally bitter.

Burlesque, the most general of these concepts, is the humorous distortion of a kind of literature, of a convention or institution, or of some kind of subject matter (a love affair, for example, or a battle). A mock epic like Pope's "Rape of the Lock" is a burlesque; it makes fun of an actual event, the stealing of a lock of a Miss Arabella Fermor's hair by one Lord Petre and the consequent uproar. Cervantes' *Don Quixote* burlesques a literary genre—the knightly romance. In both of these cases the original material, the object of the satire, though recognizable, is distorted, in order to make it ridiculous.

Parody is the similar treatment of a specific work or of the work of a specific writer. Many parodies of the style of Wordsworth and of the kind of poetry he wrote have been produced; more recently, the work of T. S. Eliot has received similar attention. Indeed there is hardly a writer with a distinctive style who has not been parodied; parody can be an indirect tribute to a writer's genius. Most often, however, it emphasizes a writer's defects rather than reproducing his whole style and method. Thus the poem recited by the White Knight in Lewis Carroll's *Through the Looking Glass* brings out the apparent inanity and self-conscious simplicity of Wordsworth at his worst:

> I'll tell thee everything I can:
> There's little to relate.
> I saw an aged aged man,
> A-sitting on a gate.
> "Who are you, aged man?" I said.
> "And how is it you live?"
> And his answer trickled through my head
> Like water through a sieve . . . .

Caricature, finally, is close to parody, but it is aimed at the physical appearance and the behavior of a person or a type. We often see caricatures in political cartoons, and sometimes in motion pictures and plays. In the movie *The Great Dictator* Charlie Chaplin played a role that caricatured Adolf Hitler, emphasizing the strutting walk, the twitching of the little black mustache, and the general air of arrogant vanity. More general caricatures are found in Dickens: Mr. Micawber and Uriah Heep, in *David Copperfield,* are famous examples of characters whose appearance and mannerisms are so exaggerated as to make them ridiculous though recognizable types. Polonius, in *Hamlet,* is another caricature, a little less farcical than Mr. Micawber, but somewhat gentler than Uriah Heep. Caricature, like other forms of satire, differs in intensity.

To round out our consideration of satire, we should acknowledge its ultimate basis: irony. Implicit, at least, in all satire is the contrast between what is normal and what is distorted in the world. By emphasizing, and usually exaggerating, particular characteristics of persons, objects, and events, satire points out where these differ from the norm, and suggests that the difference is ridiculous. Lady Bracknell in *The Importance of Being Earnest* appears so intent on insuring that a suitor for her daughter's hand is sufficiently wealthy that not only she but this particular concern of hers (and other people's) becomes ridiculous. Satire assumes a norm—social, psychological, or moral—and makes fun of the deviations from it. But, we remember, all comedy is based partly on deviation from the norm; how do we distinguish satire from other forms of comedy? We do so by the intent of the particular work: if it is aimed at objects outside of itself, that is, if it clearly implies a judgement about objects and events extrinsic to literature, it is satirical. *Gulliver's Travels,* because of its persistent preoccupation with what is right and wrong in Swift's world and the humans that inhabited it, is satirical. In contrast, the movies of the Marx Brothers and Shakespeare's "high" comedies like *Twelfth Night* are largely concerned with themselves: although we laugh at the characters and the episodes in these works, we take most of them as they are without being made to feel they should be better. Still, we cannot draw a sharp line between satire and other kinds of comedy, for they often overlap: *The Importance of Being Earnest* is both "high" comedy and satire, as are many of Shaw's plays; and some of the Marx Brothers comedies are burlesque as well as farce. These literary concepts we are discussing are almost never mutually exclusive.

SUBTLETIES AND REFINEMENTS

THE STRUCTURE OF LITERARY COMEDY

We have, above, touched on the most fundamental elements of comedy: incongruity or inconsistency and the deviation from a norm. What we should examine now, in order to understand the subtleties of the genre, is the general structure of literary comedy, that which forms the backbone of all comedy, high, low, or satirical.

We need to recognize first of all the general plot pattern of comedy, which Northrop Frye has analyzed in some detail in his *Anatomy of Criticism*. The pattern of comedy is the reverse of the tragic pattern. That of comedy demonstrates the integration of the protagonist with society.[1] Usually this process is opposed deliberately or otherwise by a group of "blocking" characters, who furnish a good deal, if not most, of the amusement in the story. This typical pattern can easily be seen in *The Importance of Being Earnest,* in which all kinds of amusing characters impede the attempts of Jack and Gwendolyn, Algy and Cecily to unite, and where almost everyone is paired off with someone else in a burst of togetherness at the end. It is also perceptible, though less explicitly, in such slapstick as that of the Three Stooges. When these serve as protagonists they invariably get into trouble with other characters; through the buffets and pratfalls that result, the stooges are restored to their proper place in society (usually at the bottom of the heap). Most often, however, these clowns—and others in the same category, like the Marx Brothers—are not the protagonists but blocking characters who get in the protagonist's way. They are usually disposed of somehow so that the story ends on a note of social har-

[1] See Frye, p. 43.

mony, but in the course of the narrative they provide us with a good many laughs.

This pattern of integration is primordial; it is the pattern from which actual comedies are derived, but it appears in different proportions in particular works. In some comedies (those, for instance, in which the Stooges, as blocking characters, remain triumphant at the end) the plot falls short of the actual integration: the world of the comic blocking characters persists, despite the efforts of the protagonists. In others, the integration is completed fairly early in the action, and more of our attention is devoted to the new world that the hero belongs to (see, for example, those musical comedies in which the boy gets the girl halfway through, and the rest of the time is spent in song and dance). The situation is analogous to that in a game, like football, golf, or chess: there is an underlying general pattern, which particular games vary in different ways.

There are, at the same time, as Frye points out, "two ways of developing the form of comedy"[2]: the emphasis can be thrown either on the blocking characters or on the achievement of the integration. The difference between the consequent two general categories is distinctive. The first is that of the more broadly humorous or the more directly and immediately interesting comedies— those, that is, which interest us because of what is going on in front of our eyes and ears rather than what is suggested or built up by the development of the plot. The second category is that of the comedies in which the plot development is more important, in which suspense is generated, in which the working out of the course of the action and of the relationships between the characters is especially interesting. Thurber's "Secret Life of Walter Mitty," and the usual Three Stooges farces are good examples of the first method of development. In Thurber's short story, we have a series of Mitty's daydreams of glory, which are wonderfully entertaining in themselves but lead to no change in the original situation or characters; in typical farces, we get a good deal of violent action

[2] p. 166.

with little plot to hang it on. In *The Importance of Being Earnest,* on the other hand, these two methods of development are used simultaneously: the witty dialogue and the amazing situations that the characters find themselves in are amusing in their own right, and at the same time we are interested in how the problems in the plot will be resolved. Indeed, no comedy of the second type is likely to be completely without immediate interest for the current action; it must be entertaining as it moves along or it will hardly be a comedy.

These, then, are the basic features of the plot of comedy. We should also recognize that comedy employs certain character types that recur over and over again, though not all of them necessarily appear in a particular work. Frye cites the "self-deprecators," the "impostors," the "buffoons," and others.[3] This kind of analysis can be very fruitful; consider the ease with which we can find examples in various periods of the types Frye cites (Falstaff, Lady Bracknell, and Groucho Marx are "impostors"; Huckleberry Finn and Jack of *Earnest* are "self-deprecators"). Indeed, certain comic types have been recognized for many, many years which fit well the categories suggested by Frye, although these conventional types are known by different names and have not been considered such broad types as Frye's. Among these conventional types are the "braggart soldier" like Falstaff, the "clever servant" who arranges and contrives events for his master's and his own benefit, and the rustic (Mortimer Snerd and Li'l Abner, for instance). We should remind ourselves, finally, that these types are commonly found combined (Walter Mitty seems to be part "self-deprecator," part "braggart soldier," for example); they are not mutually exclusive.

FORMS AND DEGREES OF COMEDY

Despite the fundamental plot pattern and the typical characters comedy varies considerably. Its basic nature is unchanging, but its forms, degrees, and methods of development differ considerably. We

[3] p. 172

have seen a little of this range in the first part of the chapter; now
we should consider this range more fully.

  If we establish a line between the extreme of tragedy and that of
comedy, to represent varying degrees of seriousness or sadness in
an elementary way, we can conceive of some of the distinctions
between various kinds of comedy. To begin with, we might recall
the types of serious, though not tragic, narrative that we noted in
the chapter on tragedy. Of these, the problem play (and similar
nondramatic works) are inherently the closest to tragedy. Next, we
list the *drame,* which is generally serious, even sentimental in tone,
but which ends happily. At this point on our scale tragedy and
comedy overlap most directly. In *drame,* often called tragicomedy
or sentimental comedy, often the only thing that prevents tragedy
is the happy ending. Indeed in many cases the action is so inherently
sad that a happy ending is obviously contrived, and we wish that
for the sake of consistency the work had ended sadly. In other,
more typical cases, the nature of the action is more ambiguous, always on the verge of the tragic, but always capable of ending happily. We often realize in these cases that everything is sure to turn
out all right at the end even though the action is generally sober, even
sad (though enjoyably so, perhaps); superficially the tone is sad,
basically it is pleasant.

  This *drame* is an exaggeration of the sentimental tendency of
"romantic comedy" (meaning in this case that it is about love, and
that it is not very realistic), which is ably represented by Shakespeare's *Twelfth Night, Much Ado About Nothing,* and *As You
Like It.* In these plays we see a fine young hero in love with a
beautiful heroine, and/or vice-versa, and we follow their adventures (most of them serious but not sad, entertaining but not
comic) in the process of being united. There is often incidental
comic byplay, usually by minor characters. Sometimes this element
looms large in the work, and the plot involving the main characters
serves merely as a kind of framework; in such cases, the work
verges on a "lower" or more farcical kind of comedy. Typically,

however, romantic comedy is not "funny" so much as "good fun." It is not realistic, but takes place in a never-never land in which the course of true love, though it may not run absolutely smooth, is sure to end satisfactorily. *The Importance of Being Earnest* burlesques this kind of comedy.

Sometimes plot in comedy is strongly emphasized and developed to the point that its ins and outs, its twists and turns and surprising events, constitute the main interest. In this case we have the "comedy of intrigue," or "situational comedy." *Earnest* once again can be cited as a parody; its interest depends partly on the intrigue of the young lovers in their attempts to get together, but many of the plot developments and situations are so improbable that they serve to poke fun at the type of comedy to which the play belongs. In the process, it illustrates many typical features of that type. The intrigue and the resulting entertaining situations that the characters find themselves in are fundamental. In addition, we can see the element of disguise in Jack's assuming the name of Earnest in the country in order to appear the properly dignified uncle to Cecily; and the clever servant who typically contrives the intrigue appears, in his function, in Algy.

At the opposite end of the scale from tragedy in almost every way are farce comedy and pure farce, the only difference between them being that farce comedy depends a little less blatantly on physical action and situation as a source of amusement, and therefore may be somewhat wittier. Farce, as we have seen, is the least serious form of comedy. It is indeed the most positively "funny," producing belly-laughs; the experience it stimulates is more nearly emotional than intellectual.

These forms overlap in many ways, as we know. There are farcical scenes even in some tragicomedies; in fact "mechanical" mixtures of various general types are common. Even more common are the works that fuse characteristics of the different types into "compounds" as *The Importance of Being Earnest* does. Charlie Chaplin demonstrated that farce can be extremely pathetic if the right light is thrown upon it: the character of the tramp for which Chaplin is famous often got himself into uproariously silly predicaments that at the same time made him appear particularly appealing (there comes to mind the scene in which he was caught in and belabored by a defective machine that had been designed to feed factory workers, such as he, automatically). Cases like the tramp's remind us in addition that even the distinction between comedy and tragedy is not always certain. What from one point of view is comic, in other words, may from another be tragic, or what is comic on the surface may on closer inspection be tragic. Classic instances of this ambiguity are to be found in ironic works or passages, such as the scene in *Oedipus Rex* in which the king makes himself almost ridiculous when he refuses to understand the prophet Tiresias and accuses him of being ignorant as well as blind, while at the same time, this behavior points to the tragic end we know is in store for the king.

Ambiguity of this kind is especially evident in the various sorts of satire. Since satire always has a point to make, it never focuses narrowly on the material of the particular narrative, but brings out as well its implications—the significance of that material in a larger frame of reference—thus encouraging the audience to consider it not only as entertainment but seriously, too. As a result, many of the different varieties of satire we are now going to examine are capable of ranging from the humorousness of farce almost to the seriousness of tragedy, depending on the degree of the intensity of the satire, despite inherent tendencies of particular varieties toward seriousness or toward humor.

To begin with, it is common to divide satire into two kinds according to intensity and tone. Strong, emphatic, even bitter and angry, satire is called Juvenalian, while more urbane, gentle, and humorous satire is called Horatian; both terms come from the names of Latin writers. In this manner we make a distinction between two very different but equally valid basic satirical attitudes, the one of anger at man's follies and vices, the other of amusement. Both attitudes are valid because, as a number of critics have pointed out, they animate all satire to some extent; satire is intended to inspire laughter at the expense of human behavior that is essentially unworthy. Whether the particular satire is Juvenalian or Horatian depends on which is emphasized more, the unworthiness of the behavior or the laughter.

Under these two general headings we find certain specific variations. First, at the most intense end of the scale, we find invective, that is, name calling, the hurling of unpleasant epithets and descriptions directly at the person guilty of misbehavior. This extreme form of satire is close to the limit of art; it can degenerate into merely unpleasant insult that is not entertaining and is not, therefore, a type of comedy at all nor indeed literary. Swift, in *Gulliver's Travels,* has the king of the Brobdingnagians characterize man as "the most pernicious race of little odious vermin that Nature ever suffered to crawl upon the surface of the earth"; although this is as close as invective can safely come to the limits of comedy, it is entertaining because of the neatness of the style and because of the implicit contrast between the opinion it expresses and the approbation that Gulliver at that moment expected, having just finished describing the European arts of war. Very close to invective, indeed overlapping it, we find sarcasm, the bitter, deliberately unpleasant, and personal satirical attack. The essential difference between invective and sarcasm is that the latter is partly ironical in method: compare "You third son of donkey's half-witted cousin!" to "You are the most blindingly brilliant, the most exquisitely perceptive . . . jackass I've met in a long time!"

Somewhere in the middle of the scale between inherently bitter satire and laughing satire we locate such realistic comedy as the "comedies of humours" and the "comedies of manners." The realism of this kind of satire, which depicts commonplace, ordinary persons and circumstances, in effect avoids the overimaginative improbability of romantic comedy on the one hand and the rather simple-minded coarseness of farce on the other. The first of these two representative comic satires, the comedy of humours, was a type of drama originally developed in English by Ben Jonson in the seventeenth century as a means of attacking common human foibles; it was based on the medieval theory that the body is composed of four substances ("humours"), and that if these were seriously out of balance some kind of eccentricity, at least, would result. Jonson's comedies ridiculed the behavior of characters dominated by some peculiarity—a desire for peace and quiet, say, or a real defect like greed or jealousy—and while this kind of drama as such lasted only a short while, its effect was felt for a long time both in the drama and also in prose fiction and poetry. We rarely see specific comedies of humours today, but we find much the same technique in a good deal of narrative (in Dickens, for instance). The comedy of manners, which developed later in the same century in England, concentrated on showing up the misconduct of high society—the loose morals, the affectation in speech and clothes, and the frivolity. Again, this kind of attack on society is still very common, indeed much more common than the "humours" attack. We have at hand an excellent example: *The Importance of Being Earnest,* again. As satire these two forms are placed in the middle of the scale because they are typically neither very bitter nor very farcical, and because, at the same time, they are capable of attaining either extreme. Anyone who reads many such comedies will see that they can be very intense, even brutal, or very relaxed and amusing.

Now we are in the part of the scale of intensity where Horatian satire is to be found, by which we mean a relatively moderate and amusing satire, as indicated before. As in the case of Juvenalian satire there is some variety within the general class. Horatian satire is always good-humored by definition, but it can be more or less good humored—that is, more or less pointed as satire. We are already acquainted with the more amusing varieties of Horatian satire, parody, caricature, and burlesque. The satire evinced in these genres is unmistakeably comic, and the comedy is broad, sometimes farcical. Man's foolishness is here genuinely made fun of rather than held up to scorn. In the last variety of Horatian satire to consider, travesty, this pleasant tone is not always the rule; travesty is usually fairly light and witty, as *Don Quixote,* for instance, often is, but it can be seriously degrading. The concept signifies debasement, treating something great and important as if it were small and insignificant. Thus, in Cervantes' novel, knights and knight-errantry become the farcical delusions of an overly idealistic old man; the tone is often broadly comic, as in the episode in which Don Quixote tilts at the windmill, but sometimes it turns bitter because of the sympathy we come to feel for the protagonist. On one level travesty is a form of burlesque, but because of the deflation inherent in it, it can become something much more cutting.

There is, as we have noted, a comic vision of the world as well as a tragic one: to those who think, life is purportedly a comedy. This serves to confirm the observation that there is an essential ingredient, or a number of ingredients, to be found in all comedy. We recognize the basic nature of comedy even in its many modified forms, and its various degrees of intensity. As with tragedy, however, we observe that works are more or less comic, rather than purely comic or not so at all; and we observe that the various combinations of the essential ingredients produce comedies that differ markedly at first glance. This consciousness of the manifold variations of essential elements is particularly necessary for a sophisticated understanding of such a general concept as comedy.

Symbolism

BASIC TERMS AND CONCEPTS

Symbolism is a whole dimension of literature. Although sometimes it is simply a means to an end in a given work, in many cases
it is in effect the whole story, providing its basic fabric. And at the
same time it is a means of our perceiving some fundamental aspects of the unity of all literature and indeed of all human experience as embodied in literature. To understand how this can be, we
must first understand what symbolism and some of its related concepts are and how they function.

GENERAL DEFINITION

Generally and abstractly, symbolism means the use (deliberate
or otherwise) of particular objects or actions to represent relatively
broad concepts. In literature, then, it would mean that the characters, settings, and events in a work represent ideas, "institutions,"
intellectual attitudes, that are broader and more significant than
the particular concrete representatives. To provide a more precise

understanding of symbolism we need to distinguish between it and related concepts, however. The easiest way to do this is to follow a progression from simple, straightforward, and familiar concepts. Let us begin with imagery.

SYMBOLISM AND RELATED CONCEPTS

Imagery in literature, as we know, is the sense-impressions, the physical sensations, represented by "concrete" words and phrases in a work, a concrete or image-making word being one which re-calls to us a physical sensation or a number of them. When we read "He was a king," we are dealing with a fairly simple relation-ship: a specific thing or person, in this case, ("He") is equated with a single physical object which presents itself to us as a visual image ("king"). Since the relationship is that of simple identity, we are often presented only with the second of the two terms of the equa-tion, as at the beginning of "Sir Patrick Spens": "The king sits in Dumferling town . . . ." From our viewpoint, this is the same as saying "There is a man. The man is a king. The king sits in . . .," but in the poem those preliminary steps are assumed. The fact that they can be assumed indicates that the image and the thing it is linked with are identical; the only difference—an important one, but one that does not concern us now—is that the second term, the image, is more vivid and particular.

At the next stage of our progression, the relationship is not so simple. This stage is that of metaphor, which we know is a selec-tive comparison rather than an equation. When we read, that is, "He was like a king," or "He was a veritable Charlemagne," we realize that "He" was not literally a king, or Charlemagne, but that "He" had some of a king's, or Charlemagne's, characteristics. The essential difference between metaphor and imagery as equations is that in imagery one thing is lined up directly with an equivalent (He → king), whereas in metaphor one thing is identified with something that is logically off to the side, as it were, though that something resembles the first term's immediate equivalent in certain ways:

$$He \diagdown \begin{bmatrix} - \rightarrow businessman(?) \\ \rightarrow king \end{bmatrix}$$

There is still a one-to-one identification just as there is in the equation set up in imagery: one unit is identified with another unit (even if the individual units are multiple, they are logically equal in scope, as in "He was a whole regiment, all by himself"). The relationship is still a direct one in this respect.

At the next stage of the progression, that of symbolism at its most mechanical, there is an important change in one of the units in the equation and in the nature of this "equation." This is the stage of "signification" of the equation by which a sign is lined up with something that it represents. The changes are these: the first unit (the sign) here has little or no intrinsic significance or value, and the relationship between the two units is a process of representation, not a simple equation. Let us consider the example of a crown, plain and unadorned, devoid of gold or jewels. Even such a crown—perhaps a circle of iron, with no value of its own—can stand for a king or for kingship. Somehow this plain band of iron seems in various circumstances to equal the king or the kingship; indeed in certain ceremonies it might be treated as if it were the king himself. Still, we know perfectly well that the two are not identical. It is only in certain circumstances, as we said, and by agreement—through our agreeing that the piece of iron will mean the king in these circumstances—that this crown has any significance. Otherwise it is merely a piece of iron, a hoop for a small keg, perhaps.

The difference between identity (as in imagery and metaphor) and signification can be illustrated by the following. Chimpanzees, it is said, can be taught to drive some kind of a vehicle and to follow rules of the road—but with one important reservation. They have difficulty distinguishing between identity and signification; to them, a red light does not *signify* "Stop," but *is* "Stop." No matter where they see one and no matter what its source, traffic light or neon light, they will stop. Fortunately it is easier for human beings to make the distinction involved. We would not say that the crown *is* a king or kingship but that it stands for it. This is the process of symbolism at its simplest level: one thing stands for something else, the relationship still being almost one-to-one. Although the sign (the crown) may stand for an idea (kingship), as our earlier general definition of symbolism would indicate, that idea is approximately a unit. Kingship may suggest various qualities, rights, and duties, but these are implied on a secondary level which is not immediately pointed to by the sign, but realized by us after some reflection. These secondary aspects, linked together, form the unified concept of kingship. A sign, then, is a rudimentary symbol, having little or no intrinsic importance, which stands typically for an object or a relatively unified idea, in approximately a one-to-one relationship.

The next stage of increasing complication, and the next to last, is that of allegory. This is a form of literary symbolism in which a structure of symbolic or "signifying" characters and objects is organized in a narrative. One of the most famous examples of allegory is John Bunyan's *Pilgrim's Progress,* a prose narrative written in seventeenth-century England, in which Pilgrim, the protagonist, sets out for the City of Zion and encounters many difficulties on the way. He is severely burdened at first by a pack on his back representing his sins, and partly for that reason has a hard time struggling through the Slough of Despond (swamp of discouragement); he is captured at one point by the Giant, Despair, and held prisoner in Doubting Castle; and later he has trouble climbing the Hill Difficulty. In such allegories the persons and objects are worked up into a structure that is largely responsible for the significance of those persons and objects and for the events that involve them. This structure, in other words, constitutes the circumstances or context in which the signs are significant: in *Pil-*

grim's Progress, we agree, a hill stands for the difficulties facing a sinner on his road to salvation, though elsewhere it is just a hill.

Allegory is not a story based on a structure simply of specific signs, however. First, we note that in allegory the signs often point to general and abstract concepts rather than to single simple things or phenomena like a king or "Stop." This is possible for signs, as we saw in the case of the iron crown's standing for kingship. In allegory, however, the signs point to abstract concepts more generally. Despair, Difficulty, and Despondency are typical enough of the kind of idea represented tangibly in allegory. Many of the signs in allegory, in other words, are not so rudimentary as a red traffic light. But at the same time, the concepts represented in allegories are likely to be simple and coherent on the immediate level, like kingship as it was represented by the crown. In allegory the signs typically point to somewhat more complex specifics than usual for signs. The second particular feature of allegory is that some of the "signs" are intrinsically meaningful, partaking to some extent of the concepts for which they stand. The Hill Difficulty in Bunyan's story is hard to climb and Pilgrim's burden weighs on him physically as sins weigh on him spiritually. In this respect these "signs" should be called symbols, since one essence of symbolism is that it derives from the very nature of the symbol itself. In other words, the Hill symbolizes Difficulty because it *is* difficult (to climb), and the Slough symbolizes despondency because one becomes psychologically mired in despondency.

Allegory overlaps on symbolism as a general literary method in narrative, for it is basically symbolic in various ways. Its symbolism operates on a more rudimentary level, however, and within a restricted scope. The concrete symbols employed in allegories, though they have in them some of the characteristics of the concepts they stand for, are typically invested with those characteristics deliberately or artificially by their context, that is, by the structure of signs and symbols of which they are a part. In Edmund Spenser's famous allegory, *The Faerie Queene,* the first character we meet, a knight, is made to represent holiness, and while it is true that this particular knight turns out to be pure in thought and deed, he would be more likely to be taken, out of the context of Spenser's epic, to stand for courage or chivalry. This sixteenth-century poem is one of the few places where a knight is made to stand for the particular quality that Spenser wanted him to stand for. When an allegorical symbol possesses significant characteristics naturally, moreover, these are usually partial or superficial. For instance, the Hill Difficulty in *Pilgrim's Progress* is a "natural" symbol to the extent that any hill is hard to climb, yet this difficulty is only physical, while the full significance of the symbol, which results from the particular context of the work, is spiritual.

As a result of this deliberate or contextual investment of meaning, allegory exists as it were on two levels, the physical or literal, and the abstract or thematic. In some parts of *The Faerie Queene,* we seem to be reading about interesting but not especially meaningful adventures of various knights, ladies fair, giants, and other exotic persons—until we are informed that all these have an ulterior significance on an abstract level. At other times the concrete action seems incoherent because a great deal of emphasis has been put on the abstract meaning, so that the physical level is overshadowed: at these times we may be acutely conscious of the abstract significance while we relegate the concrete action to the background, reading the work as an intellectual treatise rather than a piece of imaginative literature. The ideal relationship between the two levels is for the concrete narrative and the abstract significance it embodies to complement each other, neither one overshadowing the other; this relationship is achieved in much of *The Faerie Queene* and *Pilgrim's Progress*.

Next, the symbolism in allegory is restricted in scope or depth by the relative simplicity and coherence of the concepts represented on the level of immediacy usual in allegory. As indicated before, the ideas treated in allegory are simplified; they become

units that can be comprehended quickly and that retain their identity in changing circumstances. Thus, the despair that the giant
represents in *Pilgrim's Progress* is a straightforward concept. By
beating and lecturing Pilgrim (and his companion Hopeful) the
giant generates despair in them, and nothing else. It is made clear
that nothing else is to be expected—neither anger, nor resentment,
nor patient fortitude; and the way in which Pilgrim expresses his
despair shows that it is simple and unambiguous, not to be con-
fused, for example, with any legitimate misgivings Pilgrim might
have about his worthiness:

> "The life we lead now is miserable. For my part, I know not
> whether is best, to live thus or to die out of hand. My soul
> chooseth strangling rather than life, and the grave is more easy
> for me than this dungeon."

The concepts dealt with in allegory are usually just as uncompli-
cated as this. The view of human nature, of society, and of the
world presented in allegory is somewhat oversimplified. The genre
uses the basic technique of symbolism, but as a general literary
method it is thematically less complex, more specific, and more
rigidly organized.

We are now in a position to perceive clearly the elements of
symbolism. We have already defined it abstractly as the use of objects or actions to represent relatively broad concepts—ideas, intellectual attitudes, "institutions." Most important, we have seen
indirectly the two most characteristic elements of symbolism.
These are first, the fact that true symbols, as distinguished from
signs and from the typical allegorical symbols, partake intrinsically
of what they represent. Second, the concepts represented by these
symbols are typically general, complex, indeed vague and ambiguous. Let us consider our example of a crown again. This time,
however, let us imagine it as a splendid work of gold and jewels,
heavy and impressive, like the crown of England. What does it
suggest? What abstract qualities and ideas does it embody? We see
wealth, luxury, and beyond that, dignity and power; we also see (in

its weight, partly) responsibility; and if we look with a more jaundiced eye we see in the crown's massive opulence an ostentatious pride. In other words, the physical characteristics of the crown represent various abstract concepts; individually and in combination these have far-reaching representative value when they are not limited by the thematic structure to be found in allegory (the organization of the ideas on an abstract level that the concrete narrative is intended to develop).

Because symbolism can be so far-reaching and so general or pervasive, it can be very powerful in its effect; and this effect is intensified by the fact that we are often not acutely and continually conscious of the symbolic potential of the concrete objects and actions in a work. In allegory, where the abstract level of meaning has to be indicated explicitly when it does not inhere in the physical objects themselves, we are likely to know all the time that we are handling ideas as well as their concrete representatives. But in a more subtly symbolic work, the abstract significance is not spelled out so explicitly, to be held at arm's length, as it were, and considered dispassionately. Instead it creeps into our minds without being overtly noticeable, carried in by the impressions made on us by the characters, settings, and action. Symbolism is usually more powerful than allegory because it is less of a deliberate process of conveying meaning. At the same time, because of the lack of explicitness, it is difficult to say specifically and definitely what the symbols represent. They stand for many different things at the same time—that is one of the particular virtues of symbolism—and some of these may almost be contradictory; critics have often argued over the significance of the symbols in one story or another.

In practice symbolism operates in different ways; it is not always as ambiguous as suggested above. We will discuss some of these ways more systematically later, but let us note briefly now two extremes of the variation commonly observable: symbolism can be specific and explicit, on the borderline of allegory, or it can be general and implicit. The way that the successive witches' scenes in

Macbeth represent the evil in the protagonist is clear and unambiguous. The relative subtlety of the representation and the complexity of the phenomena the witch scenes represent, however, is characteristic of symbolism. They stand for evil, and also for the supernatural influences on Macbeth's career, as well as for the concomitant development of his ambition and the fatalism that governs the whole process.

One thing that makes this particular symbolism explicit is the fact that it is repeated several times in the course of the play. There are several appearances of the witches, each bearing on Macbeth's ambition and his career; in the same line, we may cite the appearance of the ghost of Macbeth's murdered rival, Banquo, as another reminder that the supernatural forces that impel Macbeth upward are evil. Such a repeated symbol or symbolic pattern is called a motif; it serves to keep before us a keynote or pervasive issue of the work as a whole.

At the opposite extreme from the cases just cited is that in which the symbolism is implicit and general, that is, in which there is little or no overt indication by the writer that any symbolic significance is intended. Let us turn to *Macbeth* again for an illustration, this time to the protagonist himself: even in the absence of specific indications by the author, we can see that Macbeth is a representative type, a symbol of the human values he embodies. He is an archetypal character—one example, that is, of a kind of character to be found through almost the whole course of literature, the unscrupulously ambitious man. In this broadly symbolic sense Macbeth's nature and career constitute a version of a "myth," a general plot pattern that is also to be found throughout literature, as suggested in Chapter 6. As a version of the basic myth of tragedy *Macbeth* represents the exiling of a superior person from society, and considering the hero's particular nature, the play represents specifically the myth of the evilly ambitious man who attains power but then loses it. This mythic and archetypal analysis, while it helps reveal the thematic significance of a work—the meaning that a writer more or less deliberately tries to develop—at the same time considers the particular work in its underlying relation to the rest of literature. Let us reconsider this approach after we have refined our understanding of the nature of symbols and of their manifestation in literary works.

SUBTLETIES AND REFINEMENTS

VARIETIES OF SYMBOLS

One fundamental distinction between kinds of symbols is generally recognized, that between natural, conventional, and private symbols. The differences between the three types have to do partly with the source of the concrete symbolic objects themselves, partly with the way the symbolic relationship is created and developed.

A "natural" symbol is one that is found in external nature—all man's physical environment except what he himself has created. Such symbols, because they exist almost independently of man, inherently represent the qualities or faculties they possess. Thus, the light- and life-giving sun is a natural symbol of inspiration, of knowledge, of vitality, of hope, and of other similar qualities; the sea is a natural symbol of mystery and profundity, of illusion and mutability; a flower, a symbol of youth, innocence, and impermanence. These natural symbols are to be found throughout literature, for they are at hand for all writers and readers: we can recall the "spot of joy," the blushing, in "My Last Duchess" with which Browning symbolizes the Duchess' beauty, sweetness, and naiveté; and in Frost's "Stopping by Woods" we see the woods at night, "lovely, dark and deep" as a symbol of peace and quiet, of refuge, and of escape.

"Conventional" symbols are those whose significance is due ultimately to an agreement (often unspoken) between men, or to the position or function of the symbol in the environment that man has himself developed. A house, thus, is a common conventional symbol of home, of security, of "belonging," of what has been called "togetherness." A dog, because of his long-accepted position as man's best friend, is a symbol of companionship, devotion, and similar qualities. More clearly conventional because they have no symbolic significance except as instruments of man's experience, are such national symbols as Independence Hall and the Liberty Bell. Independence Hall and the Liberty Bell have been invested with all that the United States means to an American because of the role they played in its history.

If natural symbols are almost universally recognized and conventional symbols next most widely known, the third variety of symbols consists of those that are least familiar. These are the "private" symbols which have been developed or deliberately created by particular persons, often specific individuals. Many families have certain musical tunes, pieces of furniture, or other familiar things which mean a great deal to them not for their own sake so much as their "sentimental"—that is, their symbolic—value: Grandpa's favorite chair, though old and unattractive, comes to stand for all that Grandpa himself means to the family; or a certain carol, because it seems to "belong" to the family, is always the first one to be sung on Christmas eve. Such symbolism can be restricted and artificial, but very effective, depending on how well we know the particular symbol. To the members of these families these symbols are very potent, even though they signify little to outsiders.

In literature, private symbols develop when a group of writers associated by a common interest comes to regard certain images or phenomena as representative of their concern. The members of the "Graveyard School" of poetry in England in the eighteenth century, including Thomas Gray ("Elegy Written in a Country Churchyard"), came to attach a good deal of rather special symbolic significance to gravestones, to the cry of owls, and to the gloom of night, for example. Private symbols are also developed deliberately by individual authors, and these symbols, if they are truly private—that is, unconnected with conventional or natural symbolic values—can be very troublesome to inexperienced readers. A famous case of a poet who developed his own set of symbols is that of the twentieth-century Irish poet William Butler Yeats. In one of his best-known poems, "The Second Coming," he describes the state of the world as follows:

> Turning and turning in the widening gyre
> The falcon cannot hear the falconer;
> Things fall apart; the centre cannot hold . . . .

Since this poem is not about falconry these opening images, and especially the statements based on them ("Things fall apart"), are puzzling. Even if we conceive of a falcon circling in a "gyre"—a rising, expanding spiral—around a falconer, we find it hard to see why this indicates that the world is coming apart. The solution lies in Yeats's semimystical, symbolic conception of the universe and of experience. According to his "Vision," as he called it, history consists of a succession of antithetical "gyres," each one originating in a supernatural birth, such as that of Helen of Troy, who was the daughter of the Greek woman Leda and the god Zeus, in the form of a swan. Each successive historical gyre would expand from its central event until it overextended itself and flew apart; then a new supernatural birth would occur to begin a new gyre. For us to comprehend "The Second Coming," thus, we must learn about Yeats's private symbolism, just as a Buddhist must learn about Christianity before he can comprehend the symbolism of the Cross.

Private symbolism can make a work obscure at first. That particular symbolism, however, will have a thematic significance that no other material could reproduce; private symbols are developed for precisely that reason. Moreover, what may be a private symbol at its first appearance often becomes an accepted convention as more and more readers become familiar with it. This is the case with Yeats's "gyre," and with some of the private symbols that T.S. Eliot created or developed out of his vast and recondite reading: some of the symbolism of the Tarot pack (an extremely ancient

deck of cards sometimes used by fortune-tellers) has become conventional since it was cited in Eliot's most famous poem, "The
Waste Land," in 1922. Many conventional symbols, after all, are
private symbols that have become widely known and are therefore
no longer private; the Cross was once a symbol meaningful to only
a few Christians.

Finally, before we examine some of the different manifestations
of symbolism in literature, let us recognize that symbols vary in
other ways than those just indicated. Some are more intense, more
powerful than others, as the American flag means more than a fra-
ternity pin; and the Cross, to a Christian, means more than a figure
of Buddha. This difference is due to experiences and the knowledge of the persons who encounter the symbols rather than to variations in the symbols themselves. Symbols differ also in their immediacy—in their degree of familiarity, the quickness with which
we recognize them—even when they are of the same general kind
(natural or conventional). The symbolic value of the earth, for example, is almost immediately perceived by everyone—most of us
are familiar with a sense of the earth's fundamental beneficence
and fruitfulness. On the other hand many of us do not so immediately regard fire as an instrument of purification, spiritual or otherwise; we can recognize in it that symbolic value, but it is not so
directly apparent to us as that of the earth. This difference, too, is
due to variations in human experience, but to more general variations. The immediacy of a symbol varies according to the reader's
cultural background, rather than to his personal experience.

VARIATIONS IN THE PRACTICE OF SYMBOLISM

We have already glanced at the actual practice of symbolism in
touching on the literary concepts of archetypes and myths and on
the general degrees of symbolic explicitness. Let us now reconsider
systematically this kind of variation and others like it.

Explicit and obvious symbolism is to be found in many different kinds of literary works; for the sake of convenience let us discuss Matthew Arnold's poem "Dover Beach." It begins:

> The sea is calm to-night,
> The tide is full, the moon lies fair
> Upon the straits;—on the French coast the light
> Gleams and is gone; the cliffs of England stand,
> Glimmering and vast, out in the tranquil bay.
> Come to the window, sweet is the night-air!
>
> Only, from the long line of spray
> Where the sea meets the moon-blanch'd land,
> Listen! you hear the grating roar
> Of pebbles which the waves draw back, and fling,
> At their return, up the high strand,
> Begin, and cease, and then again begin,
> With tremulous cadence slow, and bring
> The eternal note of sadness in.

So far we see a beautiful and peaceful night scene, for the most part, which the poet invites someone to share. The only specific hint of an ulterior significance seems to lie in the word "eternal." In the next stanza, however, Arnold writes:

> Sophocles long ago
> Heard it on the Aegean, and it brought
> Into his mind the turbid ebb and flow
> Of human misery; we
> Find also in the sound a thought,
> Hearing it by this distant northern sea.

These lines make it clear that the night scene is intended to be symbolic. In the third stanza Arnold specifies what it represents:

> The Sea of Faith
> Was once, too, at the full . . . .

The ebbing tide is thus symbolic of the ebbing religious faith in the world. Indeed the symbolism is so specific here that were it not developed, amplified, and modified later in the course of the poem we might call it allegorical, or even metaphorical.

At the other extreme we find works in which the symbolism is almost thoroughly implicit—in which, as we said before, there is little overt indication that any symbolism is intended. In the absence of such overt indication experienced readers will recognize representational elements in various characters or objects while less sophisticated readers will find none. This is what happens with *Gulliver's Travels:* most children lack the experience necessary to perceive what Swift was really writing about (although they enjoy Gulliver's adventures) while adults can perceive the satiric significance. What we may consider "implicit" symbolism is the kind found in Mark Twain's *Huckleberry Finn;* there is so little indication of symbolic intention there in that it is very often taken primarily as an adventure story, albeit one that raises certain social and personal issues. Yet we can see that fundamentally the characters and events in the narrative are broadly representative, that is, symbolic. A similar case, an interestingly debatable one, is Frost's "Stopping by Woods." The concluding stanza reads:

> The woods are lovely, dark and deep.
> But I have promises to keep,
> And miles to go before I sleep,
> And miles to go before I sleep.

The question here is whether the woods are symbolic, and if so, of what? We have suggested that they symbolize peace and quiet, escape, even irresponsibility; this is suggested by the contrast between the description of the woods and the line that follows, and while this symbolism is implicit rather than overt, it is clear. If we go further, as some critics have, and take the poem to embody a kind of a death wish, seeing the dark and deep woods as a symbol of attractive death, we are less certain about the symbolism.

In this case, the symbolism is quite implicit; it can be seen by perceptive readers, but it is not indicated overtly.

Usually the symbolism in a given work is neither so obvious as in "Dover Beach" nor so latent as in "Stopping by Woods"; usually we are made to realize the existence of the symbolism but without having its significance spelled out for us in detail. This is the case in Shelley's sonnet "Ozymandias":

> I met a traveller from an antique land
> Who said: "Two vast and trunkless legs of stone
> Stand in the desert. Near them, on the sand,
> Half sunk, a shattered visage lies, whose frown,
> And wrinkled lip, and sneer of cold command,
> Tell that its sculptor well those passions read
> Which yet survive, stamped on these lifeless things,
> The hand that mocked them and the heart that fed.
> And on the pedestal these words appear—
> 'My name is Ozymandias, king of kings:
> Look on my works, ye Mighty, and despair!'
> Nothing beside remains. Round the decay
> Of that colossal wreck, boundless and bare
> The lone and level sands stretch far away."

It is clear that the ruined statue is symbolic; although the poet does not tell us so, we can perceive it from the fact that the statue is singled out, pointed at, and described portentously. And we can perceive that the statue is a symbol of futile pride, although the poet does not say so, from the contrast between the ruins and the inscription. Though the symbolism here is implicit, it is clear to a moderately perceptive and experienced reader. We feel sometimes that an author is being obscure in refusing to be more explicit, but after all, we would not want to be led like children to see the symbolic significance of a literary work; moreover, if that significance were stated too explicitly, the work would no longer be a piece of imaginative literature but a lecture. What is most important, the significance of a symbol ultimately resides in the symbol itself and cannot be adequately stated explicitly.

Another noticeable difference in the manifestation of symbolism is in its pervasiveness in a given work. Some works, that is, are thoroughly and continuously meaningful on a symbolic level, while in others symbols appear only occasionally. If a work is persistently symbolic the symbolism is obviously important; occasional symbols may be relatively incidental or they may be crucial in some respect. We might think there would be some correlation between the pervasiveness and the degree of explicitness, but we cannot count on this, for there have been many thoroughly symbolic works whose significance has had to emerge without the least word on the subject from the writer, and conversely many incidental symbols in literary works have been explicitly indicated.

Conrad's *Heart of Darkness* will illustrate well how impressive a pervasively symbolic work can be. In that narrative, we follow the adventures of Marlow in Africa on two levels simultaneously all the time; we are active both imaginatively and intellectually during the whole course of the narrative, and while we watch the particular events of this story we also have our eyes on the rest of humanity, seen through those events. The experience has a very rich ambiguity.

For examples of occasional symbolism, let us examine "Stopping by Woods" on the one hand, and "My Last Duchess" on the other. The first shows us the use of a single symbol in a central position in a poem, while the second lets us see a more incidental use. Frost, by the "woods," represents an absolutely fundamental concept, one without which the poem would be totally different. At the end of Browning's dramatic monologue, on the other hand, in the statue of "Neptune taming a sea-horse" that the Duke points out to his visitor, we have an example of an incidental symbol that serves to re-emphasize concepts already clearly brought out—the Duke's pride, and his desire to dominate. The poem would suffer if this symbol were omitted or changed, but its general theme would remain the same.

The two kinds of variations in the practice of symbolism (in explicitness and in pervasiveness) that we have just discussed are important to the particular symbolic works and to the critical analysis of them. The next consideration of symbolism also involves us in the character of particular works and their analysis, and at the same time it involves us in the basic theory of symbolism and indeed of literature as a whole. The symbolism in literary works may vary in particularity; on one level it is specific, obvious, and immediate while at the same time it may be equally significant but on a different level, a "deeper" one. On the one hand we have to consider the immediate symbolism for a full comprehension of a given work, while on other occasions, or even at the same time, we will consider the more fundamental symbolism in a work in a wider perspective. There is an important difference, that is, between the superficial (though potent) symbolism of "Dover Beach" or "Ozymandias" and the level of symbolism we touched on in our comments on the archetypal and mythic significance of Macbeth as a tragic hero.

Let us first take the case of a work in which symbolism is one of the primary methods of thematic development, "Ozymandias." Here we cannot ignore the symbolism, for it has been specifically developed and immediately related to the particular point of the poem. The "frown, / And wrinkled lip, and sneer of cold command," and the inscription on the statue's base do not merely vaguely suggest pride and arrogance and other attributes of tyranny but clearly make the ruined statue embody those characteristics, as well as indicate that they exist more generally. Essential to the poem, therefore, is the idea that the statue is not an isolated piece of broken-down antiquity, but a symbol.

This kind of particularity is encountered in many literary works; we have seen it in the sea in "Dover Beach" and in the statue of Neptune in "My Last Duchess." We can also see it in much more casual forms, like a given character's clothes or house; though we may not notice these symbols at once, we know that they have an immediate part to play in the development of the narrative. But there is a considerable difference between this level of symbolism and that on which we conceive of Oedipus and Hamlet as the same character.

On this "secondary" or deeper level we aim at an understanding of a literary work not by analyzing it in isolation, but by applying to it our knowledge of all literature, by considering it as a part of the total pattern of literature. In the process, we will put the particular work on the same plane as other similar works, rather than keeping it in the forefront of our attention; the change in our perspective means that our increased understanding of it will accompany and result from our wider consideration of literature. This wider consideration is worth undertaking for its own sake; let us here suggest some of its bases and elements.

Earlier in this chapter we mentioned that Macbeth and his career are to be seen as archetype and myth, that is, as a kind of character persistently to be found in literature, and a similarly persistent pattern of events. The basis for this analysis lies in the observation by various scholars that the ancient myths—Greek, Hebrew, Egyptian, and others—are not old fantastic stories about supernatural beings and strange events that nobody believes in any more, but symbolic manifestations of human nature and behavior that are still present in one form or another. For instance, we still consider the sequence of the seasons a kind of life and death cycle, as if the earth were reborn every spring, matured during the summer, and died slowly during the fall and the winter; this pattern is exactly what is embodied in many ancient myths. In the Greek myth of Persephone we see an expression of the same cycle: that goddess, the wife of the ruler of Hades, reputedly returned to spend half of every year on the surface of the earth; the half she spent in Hades is autumn and winter, while the other half is spring and summer. In all such cases the myth is an expression (not an "explanation") of some facet of human experience, and the fact that we no longer believe in the existence of certain forms of an archetype or in particular myths does not mean that what they represent has little significance to us. On the contrary, what these myths represent, these basic elements of human life, have been reproduced in many different cultures and different ages up to the present (we can regard the popular songs about youth and love and

flowers in the springtime as a kind of mythic expression of the re-
birth of the year).

The implications of this observation for literature are far reach-
ing and complex; we can summarize them as follows. In the first
place it has become evident that almost all of our literature, of the
past and the present, is composed of various versions and combinations of archetypes, and that it constitutes in an important sense
various versions of familiar myths. On one level, that is, a great
deal of literature consists of the same characters involved in the same
events, though these appear in many different guises. We need only
remind ourselves of the number of times the handsome young hero
has met and eventually won the beautiful maiden in the history of
human literature. For a somewhat less obvious case, we can cite
the numbers of times the Oedipal son-mother relationship has appeared: the son overly devoted to a loving mother and resentful of
his father has appeared in *Oedipus Rex* itself, in *Hamlet,* and more
recently in D. H. Lawrence's *Sons and Lovers,* to select cases
widely scattered in time. Scholars and critics recognize the existence of these myths and archetypes in literature; the problem now
is to identify and to correlate them, to analyze the relationship between them, to organize the material so that it can help us perceive
clearly more of the fundamental nature of literature (Northrop
Frye's *Anatomy of Criticism* should be mentioned in this connection).

We, too, should be concerned with this problem, for perceiving
the mythic and archetypal elements in some sort of organized form
will help us to understand the nature of literature better. When we
understand the archetypal pattern of comedy or tragedy, for example, we have a more precise conception of the essential nature of
these genres despite the variety of shapes they take. In dealing
with particular works, moreover (if we desire a more "practical"
value), we can distinguish between the traditional or conventional
elements and the "original" elements and see the relations between

them. It can be argued, of course, that such an understanding of this level of symbolism is hardly necessary to an immediate comprehension and appreciation of literary works, because we can perceive the "particular" symbolism without considering the mythic and archetypal relationships, and because we feel the effect of this "secondary" symbolism even if we cannot recognize it. But relying on our untutored sensibilities to feel the effect of this symbolism limits us severely, imposing narrow restrictions on the depth of our understanding, and limiting ourselves to the "particular" symbolism would be rather like treating the King James Bible as an original composition of 1611.

Finally, for a specific illustration of the difference between the immediate and the "secondary" levels of symbolism, let us recall "My Last Duchess" once again. Here we have a cruel Italian Renaissance duke who makes it clear to an envoy from the father of his prospective second wife that the first duchess was killed because she was too simple and innocent. On an immediate level, as we noted, there is a specific and immediate symbol in the last lines of the poem:

> . . . Notice Neptune, though,
> Taming a sea-horse, thought a rarity,
> Which Claus of Innsbruck cast in bronze for me!

The statuette not only suggests the duke's pride in his possessions, but also symbolizes the relationship he desires with any wife of his. Now, however, if we hold the poem at arm's length and consider the general nature of the characters and the events they take part in, in relation to the rest of literature, we can see that the duke and his last duchess are rather familiar archetypes, symbols of evil power on the one hand and of innocent good will on the other. In the destruction of the duchess by the duke we have one version of a mythic pattern of events that can be found in many literary works. Going back some two hundred and fifty years from Browning's poem, we find that Shakespeare's *Romeo and Juliet* embodies essentially the same myth in the destruction of the young lovers by the deadly feud between their families, the manifestation of an evil social force that they cannot withstand. And going even further back, we find in the seduction of Eve by Satan the same kind of defeat of innocence by evil power; as seen in Milton's *Paradise Lost* of the late seventeenth century, Satan and Eve are similar in important ways to Browning's duke and duchess, though hardly on the same plane.

We do not "need" to recognize this "secondary" symbolism in order to read Browning's poem; but recognizing it does broaden and deepen our understanding of it, and it is certainly necessary to a thorough understanding of literature, of which it is a part.

In sum, symbolism in all its dimensions must be studied because it is a basic element in most literary works whether it is deliberately or specifically employed as a technique or not. The study of literary symbolism, though more immediately appropriate in relation to certain works than to others, is a valid and profitable approach to all literature.

9 ⚬⚬⚬⚬⚬⚬⚬⚬⚬⚬⚬

Convention

BASIC TERMS AND CONCEPTS

In this chapter we are going to consider certain aspects of literary criticism and theory. We will attain a wide perspective on literature by considering literary works not as individual artistic creations by particular persons but rather in their relation to the history and development of literature and in relation to formal and psychological principles that govern it. Our immediate object will be to discuss elements of the study of literature rather than to discuss elements of literature itself. Our wider perspective will be achieved by setting ourselves at a slightly further remove from literary works than before.

BASIC DEFINITIONS

Generally, we are now considering literature in relation to the principal conventions that govern it. The first thing to do is to make clear what is meant by "conventions." A literary convention, like any other convention, is a procedure generally accepted or followed simply because it *is* generally accepted or followed. There may be different reasons why various conventions develop in the first place, but it is when they are firmly established and widely accepted that they become conventions. Consider the fact that the audience in a theater is allowed to see into a room, one of whose walls has been removed—this common stage set has become a convention. Nowadays we are so accustomed to this convention that we are rarely conscious of it and therefore find little wrong with it. Yet it would seem strange, if not ridiculous, to an ancient Greek accustomed to seeing on the stage of an outdoor amphitheater only the kind of action that could take place outdoors. To pretend that the audience could see through walls, or that walls were removed for their convenience, would not be conventional for him. It can further be seen that this convention is not strictly necessary even on our indoor stages when we recall that a good many theaters now are "in the round," or open on all sides, so that the audience surrounds the stage. Anyone who goes to a theater in the round for the first time, though very conscious at first of the change, quickly adapts himself to the new convention.

Practically all literature is governed by some conventions. Some of these are minor and incidental, like beginning each line of verse with a capital letter, and some are basic, like the plot in a novel. Some have clear and specific reasons for existing, as do soliloquies in drama (to reveal the characters' thoughts), while some are convenient techniques or devices that can be replaced by others, like the room-with-a-wall-missing stage set in our theater. It is important to realize that they are present, however, both to increase our general understanding of the nature of literature, and also because these conventions often add up to a set of "rules" that help determine the character of particular works, and at the same time provide the readers or audience with a comfortable framework that they can relate the works to. In the rest of this chapter we shall examine some of the most important general kinds of conventions, that is, areas of widely accepted literary theory in which the nature and the effects of convention are profound or especially problematical.

REALISM

First, let us consider a convention that is now so widely assumed that it seems to us not a convention but an inherent element of normal literature: realism. When we speak of realism here, we mean a general tendency or possibility in all literature rather than the consequent literary movement that arose for a time in Europe and America in the nineteenth century. Realism as we are dealing with it is the principle of representing real life accurately in literature, or at least of making it seem to be accurately represented. The literary movement based on this convention is a case in point because it particularly emphasized the representation of middle-class people and their everyday existence. The intention evidently was to avoid the fantastic, the extravagant, and the exotic—in other words to be "realistic"—and we should note that this was a conscious movement, a deliberate development of a convention rather than a blind following of a natural tendency. The literary movement was a particular application of the principle of realism, and the direction it took helps us to see that that principle is largely conventional.

Realism as a general principle means two things, one implied by the other. First, it means that the subject matter of imaginative literature should be "real life" and second, therefore, it means that the subject matter must be "true to life"—an accurate representation of real life. Obviously it would seem to follow that if a novelist, for instance, is going to make the characters, the action, and the settings realistic, he has to do so by making them accurate reflections of life. Thus Hemingway, having decided to tell the story of an attempted killing in the United States (instead of writing an ode in honor of the Greek god Zeus, let us say), presents us with an accurate picture of a small-town diner as setting, and shows us the killers behaving like real gunmen and the innocent bystanders behaving as normal people caught in their situation would behave, some trying to stay uninvolved, some indifferent, some concerned about the intended victim (see Hemingway's short story "The Killers").

Let us examine these two facets of realism in order to see more clearly what they entail. The assumption that literature should, or does, imitate life is based on the idea that literature is a part of life in a quite narrow sense, that imaginative works have little validity except as a means of letting us see the world around us more clearly, and therefore that as works of art they must be judged according to the success of their representation of life. Most of us now consider it normal for literature to imitate life fairly closely. The plays and movies we go to, the novels and stories we read, are devoted to reproducing the world and the people we know. Fairy stories have little currency now, even among children.

At the same time, however, we can recognize that this preference is a convention which writers do not always follow, and which can be set aside in favor of other conventions. We can see that literature is not so closely tied to "real" life; we know that an unrealistic work can be a masterpiece, as is Shakespeare's *The Tempest,* in which a shipwrecked king and his court find themselves in the power of the magician who rules an island and his supernatural servants. In some science fiction, too, the world as we know it is lost to sight, and we find ourselves in a never-never land which has no more relevance to the real world than had Brobdingnag, Swift's land of giants in *Gulliver's Travels,* to eighteenth-century England. In fact, when we are placed among creatures on a planet in another galaxy with no human characters at hand, we are rather further from our world than Gulliver was from Swift's. And other less familiar cases of literature divorced from life can be cited: consider the surrealist and the symbolist movements in literature, in which the intention was to reproduce not external life but the writer's psyche, his subconscious. The results, interesting though they were as experiments, were hardly "realistic"; Yeats's phrase "perne in a gyre," which we discussed in Chapter 8, illustrates the result of one writer's attempt to reproduce a part of his psychic vision. The belief that the proper subject for imaginative literature is the life that we can see around us, then, should be recognized as a convention. Although it reflects the fact that a writer cannot create his material out of thin air and imagination, but has to draw partly on his own, or others' experience, a high degree of realism, or what we may call direct realism, is somewhat artificial, as all conventions are, and raises various problems which we shall have to consider later.

The second facet of realism, that which insists on accuracy in the depiction of life, is the more obvious one at the present time. We seem to accept almost automatically the idea that literature must be based on life; we rarely think about it specifically. What we are more conscious of is the question of just how true to life a particular work is, or should be. In order to understand this question, and the particular applications of it, let us first make a distinction between two kinds of "truth to life."

In the first place, this accuracy of representation can mean historical realism, truth to the observable or verifiable facts of external life. For instance, when a clock is referred to in *Julius Caesar,* we know that Shakespeare violates the convention of historical realism because in point of fact there were no clocks in ancient Rome. And if a novelist today were to represent a tiger hunt in the wilds of Africa, his readers would no doubt throw down the book in disgust, exclaiming, "But there are no wild tigers in Africa— they live in India." Or, finally, to show that this convention governs fictional events of the future as well as those of the past and the present, let us imagine what our reaction would be if we encountered a scene supposedly a hundred years from now in which a skyscraper suddenly sprouted wings and took off into the air. Conceivable, perhaps, considering recent and possible future advances in technology, but not an accurate picture of what is really likely to occur. The question of historical realism, then, boils down to this: "Did it happen that way; is that actually the way it is; or could that happen—is it physically possible?"

Second, truth to life can mean psychological realism, truth to the way people really think, feel, and behave. If we complain that a hero is too good to be true, or that a villain is so thoroughly evil that he seems improbable, we are applying the conventional standard of judgment of psychological realism. This kind of complaint has been made about the Duke, as improbably callous, and his last Duchess, as too innocent, in Browning's poem. Readers have even turned against poor Fortunato in Poe's "The Cask of Amontillado," feeling that "nobody could be *that* stupid." And to refer to future events again, we should note that this convention of psychological realism governs more reliably there than historical realism: we seem to be safer in assuming that the way people think and act is not very likely to change radically. As a matter of fact, we even expect beings from another planet, in science fiction, to be true to human nature: an interesting manifestation of the egocentricity of the human race.

That imaginative literature ought to be accurate in its depiction of places, things, and people is thus a common basic assumption. Yet we can see that this, too, is a convention that is willingly ignored in many circumstances. It is ignored in musical comedy, and opera, where the characters burst into song, or even begin to dance singly or in groups on the slightest provocation; the audience does not object because a different convention is operating. Much poetry, similarly, is highly inaccurate as a representation of the way people talk or think—the rhythm of our speech and thought is more erratic, and the imagery and figurative language less vivid, one might say—yet people do read poetry without discomfort, having substituted the conventions of that genre (literary form) for the convention of realism. And there are other literary techniques and devices, even some supposedly employed in the service of realism, that are implicitly far from realistic. We have mentioned the boxlike stage of our conventional theaters; we can also cite the omniscient point of view in narrative fiction, for we are even less likely to be able to see into a person's mind than we are to see into a room from the outside. It is physically possible to remove the wall of a room, but we cannot read a man's mind. For this reason, no doubt, some "realistic" writers have systematically employed the objective point of view, yet many others have relied on their readers to accept the convention of omniscience as one means of achieving a degree of psychological realism not otherwise attainable.

Many readers will object at this point that the cases cited above cannot completely destroy our faith in realism because what we expect in literature is the appearance of reality, or verisimilitude, not actual experience. The conventional stage, though unrealistic, nevertheless *seems* real; and an unmitigated villain can be made believable in a literary work even though he may be an impossibility. These objections are perfectly valid. Art, by definition, is never literally realistic, as we can see if we carry the doctrine of realism to an extreme: were a tragic hero really to die in front of our eyes or a comic hero actually to run off with another man's wife, the result would not be art and our emotions and our moral sensibilities would be affected too directly. Literature, as an art, is always at one remove from real life, for complete realism is neither possible nor desirable. Our concern, therefore, has actually been with the *illusion* of reality, with verisimilitude or probability.

Recognizing that art is an imitation of life rather than "real" life itself still leaves us with the question of just how closely and accurately literature should imitate life. Moreover, there are different levels of realism, and different circumstances, that determine whether a strict adherence to the conventions of realism is desirable. We will consider later some of the problems in which these variables are manifested.

GENRES

The references above to the techniques of drama, of narrative fiction, and of poetry will have already indicated that these literary forms, or "genres," as they are called, are matters of convention. The basic idea of establishing preconceived literary forms and of predetermining the characteristics that particular kinds of works must have is very largely conventional. Although it is founded on the fact that the various kinds of imaginative activities embodied in literature find appropriate expression in different ways, the detailed application of this fact produces sets of conventions. Carrying out the consequences of this fact results in "generic" (from "genre") characteristics that are both artificial and natural at the same time.

The first, and the broadest, generic distinction that we should make is between prose and poetry, for although these shade into each other sometimes, there are fundamental differences between them. Prose, typically, is more logically coherent and restrained in phrasing, and in poetry the language is relatively rhythmical as well as vivid in its imagery. Nevertheless, prose and poetry are media rather than genres. They are means of expression rather than forms into which that expression may be shaped; these means have certain innate characteristics and certain conventional ones, but they may be used in many different situations and for many different purposes. The distinction between them is not so much between forms of art as between frames of mind, attitudes, or tones. Thus some poems are more "poetic" than others—short lyrics are more poetic than long didactic poems—and some prose is more "prosaic," as Hemingway's is, compared to Conrad's vivid and rhythmical style. The situation is a little like that involving colors and clothes: we may distinguish between bright colors and darker ones, but both of these may be used by a woman in sports wear, in daytime clothes, and in evening clothes.

The basic true genres are today most commonly taken to be narrative, the drama, and the lyric. The telling of a story in writing, the presentation of persons and events "on stage," and the representation of personal thoughts and feelings—these are the general forms into which imaginative literature falls. The elemental differences between them are evident. Briefly, narrative is at a further remove from actual events than drama, though they both deal in some way with people and action, and narrative therefore seems inherently to emphasize the pattern and significance of the events more than drama. Drama, conversely, is more immediate; it presents events as they actually occur, though selected and arranged. And the lyric, most familiar in the form of short poems, is concerned primarily with an individual's observations, meditations, imaginative speculations, and emotions. These three genres evidently correspond to basic imaginative activities; they are those in terms of which most writers and readers are inclined to think. Yet particular literary works in one genre or another borrow often from the others. Novelists and short-story writers often try to make the events in their narratives as dramatic as possible, even going so far as to adopt an objective point of view; and dramas and lyrics sometimes tell or imply coherent successions of events. The imaginative activity of a particular writer is not always completely satisfied by the opportunities offered in only one of these genres. Still, the narrative,. dramatic, and lyrical activities are basically different enough to have resulted in distinct genres.

Within the general genres there are various commonly recognized subdivisions. Most of the important ones in our time are familiar. Narrative is now usually in prose, and appears as novel or short story, or somewhere between; drama is conventionally divided into tragedy and comedy, melodrama and farce (unless these last are considered variations of the first two), and the lyric is made up of a number of different kinds of short poems, some with specific forms (such as the sonnet) and some not. As far as this outline goes it is more or less accurate, for the genres mentioned are, at the present, important and common. Yet it is incomplete in a number of ways. It ignores the great epics of the past. We know, too, that in drama there are certain genres (such as "drames" and "problem plays") somewhere between tragedy and comedy that are very common now; and similarly, the outline makes no mention of the various kinds of satire—are these to be considered varieties of lyrics, or should they be lumped partly under narrative? We cannot undertake here a thorough analysis or even an enumeration of the various genres presently recognized, let alone those no longer current; for this we must turn to a dictionary of literary terms. Later, we will have to consider some of the complexities and subtleties of the general concept of genres, but for a basic understanding of it, we must note the following four points in addition to those made above.

First, let us acknowledge that although many particular genres can be rigidly defined and neatly classified, just as many, perhaps, overlap conventional boundaries, combining characteristics of genres usually considered distinct. This is the case with satire, as noted above, which often mixes narrative and lyric, and is also embodied in drama.

Second, since all genres are largely conventional they are not now considered prescriptive so much as descriptive. That is, the size and shape of a genre—indeed, its very existence—is a matter of convenience, not of law. Writers are not obliged to follow the "rules" for a genre any more than they are obliged to wear certain clothes for certain occasions, such as a business suit for a visit to their bank or formal clothes for a dinner party or a dance; as we know, the "rules" that were once thought to dictate the proper attire are not necessarily binding. Just as the rules for clothing can be, and have, changed, so the genres may be, and are, modified. Many particular works are variations of a genre: some sonnets have no rime scheme at all, some novels (Somerset Maugham's *Moon and Sixpence,* for instance, which is based on the life of the French painter Gauguin) are not entirely fictional, and in at least some drama (such as Eugene O'Neill's *Strange Interlude*) the characters are made to turn directly to the audience and tell it what they are thinking.

Third, therefore, genres are not immortal or immutable. Some die (the literary epic, like *Paradise Lost,* has done so, in effect), some are created (the short story was born in the nineteenth century), and most are modified over a period of time.

Finally, as we must realize by now, it is not really necessary to think in terms of these conventional genres at all in order to write or read literature. There are other valid systems of genre classification besides this common one. We may note, for instance, that literary works are often categorized according to the type of audience expected, being labeled "popular" or "commercial" on the one hand, and "artistic" on the other. And as we shall note later when we consider some of the refinements of this concept, there have recently been undertaken more searching attempts to determine basic genres from other points of view.

CLASSICISM AND ROMANTICISM

The last concepts that we shall discuss under the heading of "convention" are classicism and romanticism. It is appropriate for us to do so for two particular reasons, each derived from a different basic conception of the terms.

It is well, in the first place, for us to recognize more explicitly that literary works appear in a chronological framework, that we cannot always treat them as if they were all written at the same time, to be dealt with in static theoretical terms. We have touched on this chronology now and then, as when we noted that some genres died and some were created, but in dealing with Classicism, Neo-Classicism, and Romanticism (note the capitals here) as literary movements, we will concern ourselves with some of the differences and similarities between successive literary periods, thereby emphasizing the chronological pattern in literary history.

In the second place, when we take classicism and romanticism as two (perhaps even *the* two) basic attitudes toward human experience we are dealing with the bases for most of the conventions and, indeed, many of the literary elements in this book. First, however, let us review the two literary periods.

Classicism, most succinctly, is the period name applied to the literature of ancient Greece and Rome; Neo-Classicism is that of parts of the seventeenth, eighteenth, and nineteenth centuries in France, Germany, and England; and Romanticism applies to the literature, in the same countries, of the late eighteenth and the first part of the nineteenth century. In America, the period just before and during the Civil War is often called the Romantic. What distinguishes these periods is a complex combination of intellectual and attitudinal characteristics. A general tendency in motivation, in likes and dislikes, in reasoned beliefs and unreasoned assumptions, produced in these periods enough of a recognizable pattern for us to label them, although those labels are inevitably oversimplifications.

Let us take the Neo-Classic and the Romantic periods in England as illustrations. In the first we find such writers as Dryden, Pope, Swift, and Samuel Johnson, all of whom generally admired the literature of the Greek and Roman Classic period (hence our name for their own era), and who endorsed and manifested in their work the views and characteristics they found in that period, and certain other generally consistent characteristics. To represent this complex of tendencies, let us cite their admiration of common sense, and of order, control, and restraint in literary form and style, and their conviction that human nature and experience is fundamentally uniform, so that the eccentric and exotic have relatively little place in their literature. The Romantic period can be represented by Wordsworth, Coleridge, Byron, Shelley, and Keats, not to mention the novelist and poet Sir Walter Scott. These writers, often in conscious revolt against the excesses of Neo-Classicism, argued for, and evinced in their work, a faith in spontaneity and inspiration; a desire for novelty, for variety, and for freedom from "artificial" restriction; and a belief that individuality is the keystone of all experience worth writing about.

It is easy to contrast these two movements because one followed and reacted against the other. In fact, they are not as sharply distinct as the common generalizations suggest. The "heroic couplet," which in the hands of Pope became the prototypical verse form of Neo-Classicism because of its neat symmetry and restraint, is not the only one used in the period, nor even the most common (it is outnumbered by blank verse, a form generally considered more compatible with Romanticism). And not all Romantic poetry is about nature, the supernatural, or the poet's psyche: one of Wordsworth's most famous sonnets ("Upon Westminster Bridge") is specifically about a city, London; furthermore, we should note how popular the restrictive and traditional sonnet was among these supposedly individualistic poets. While we recognize the progression from the Neo-Classical period to the Romantic, we should remember that a classification by general tendency is a simplification of a complex situation.

This realization, however, should not prompt us to ignore the reality of the general tendencies manifested in the two periods. Classicism and romanticism represent general attitudes toward experience, if not basic philosophies, as we indicated earlier. To identify these basic attitudes let each of us examine our own predilections. In ourselves we no doubt can recognize both romantic and classical sympathies. Some of the characteristics of the Romantic or the Neo-Classical period may have "rung a bell" within us; those characteristics are of course aspects of a general attitude toward life. To sum up, we say that the classicist places his faith in ordinary unglamorized life as it is, in a moderate attempt to deal with life steadily, and in a conviction that the typical and the universal in experience is the most reliable basis for his conception of the nature of things. The romantic, conversely, may be said to value individuality (as noted above) and to conceive of life and experience as a realm of potentiality not to be stultified by overinsistence on the normal; he would be likely to think in terms of movement, of dynamics, of progress, whereas the classicist would think perhaps in terms of structure and pattern. The reader can find these or similar characteristics in himself as illustration. Most probably, he will see some aspects of both tendencies in himself at the same time; almost no one is completely classic or romantic.

It follows that neither attitude is completely dominant in any literary period. Throughout the history of literature we can see both tendencies manifested: on the one hand, there is a respect for tradition and for convention, and an intense interest in conscious artistry and its products; on the other, there is a passion for experimentation and novelty, and an appreciation for the results of "inspiration" and spontaneity. We can use these concepts of classicism and romanticism as general guides to the history of literature and as a framework of philosophical conventions within which we can locate literary works. We can also use them as a basis on which to distinguish the varying manifestations of the literary elements which we have been examining, and therefore, of course, as a means of sharpening and deepening our perception of the nature of individual literary works.

SUBTLETIES AND REFINEMENTS

THE VALIDITY OF CONVENTIONS

The question that overrides all specific considerations of various conventions is that of their validity: are the conventions natural or artificial; are they genuinely valuable or not in our consideration of the nature of literature? The problem in general terms, in other words, is about the extent to which conventions are reflections or manifestations of the nature and the limits of literary work—of the fact that literature is art—and to what extent they are simply mat-

ters of tradition. There are no simple answers to the problem here
or anywhere else. The important thing now is to be familiar with
this problem as it applies to the key concepts that we are dealing
with.

THE DEGREES AND THE MANIFESTATIONS OF REALISM

The basic concern with regard to realism and the illusion of it, a
concern that has been evinced ever since Aristotle, is about the degree to which realism is necessary in literary works and about the
ways in which it manifests itself. Granted that a literary work
must be based on reality ultimately, just how realistic does it have
to be; and just how, in actual practice, is it made to be realistic?

A specific first problem concerns the focus of realism. One bone
of contention between the Neo-Classicists and the Romantics was
the question of particular truth or general truth: the Neo-Classicists maintained that only what is generally true, what is typical
rather than individual or eccentric, should be represented in literature. Truth, it is said, is stranger than fiction; unusual or coinci-
dental events are sometimes established as fact, yet if they were to
appear in a literary work, they would seem unrealistic. For instance, it actually happened during the Civil War that two brothers, one in the Union army and the other in the Confederate, met
face to face on the battlefield; in a fictional narrative, however, this
occurrence would seem improbable. What is probable, rather than
simply possible, should be respresented in literature, it is argued,
for the proper function of literature is to permit us to understand
our world and our experience as it normally is. The opposing argument says that life is not so dull, that it is really full of surprises
and coincidences, and even if it weren't, literature should liberate
our imaginations in order to help our spirits achieve some kind of
supramundane experience. This dispute, like many others, resolves
itself partly into the opposition between basic assumptions about
the nature and function of literature: is it fundamentally instruction

as the classical attitude suggests, or is it more nearly inspiration as romanticism feels it to be?

A second problem for us emerges from the fact that in actual practice it is the degree of realism that is uncertain, not the focus. Even if critics agree that literature should be realistic, they often disagree on the question of just how realistic it should be: some argue that literature should approach life as nearly as possible, some maintain that literature need only suggest reality, and some feel that there is no necessary connection of art with external experience at all. This range is reflected in various particular problems, as the following questions will indicate. Should literature present "slices of life," without arranging or emphasizing the components for "artistic" purposes? Should such arrangement and emphasis be permitted as long as it does not distort "normal" life? Can all kinds of artistic techniques and devices be allowed if they are made to seem real or probable for the moment? Is it possible, at the extreme of unrealism, to have completely "abstract" art in literature? Are we to rule out *Gulliver's Travels* and other science fiction because they are not realistic enough; are we going to condemn the transparent stage sets that let us see the action inside and outside a house at the same time, as in Arthur Miller's *Death of a Salesman?* Are we going to accept literature as "imaginary gardens with real toads in them," to quote Marianne Moore, a modern American poet; that is, if we accept the world depicted in literature even when it is obviously a piece of invention and perhaps quite "unrealistic," will we find that the objects and events in it actually have just as much validity in terms of the real world as those in real life itself? If we accept *Gulliver's Travels,* that is, will we find that the Lilliputians are very like real people? And even if this is so, what is our verdict on the Yahoos: are they just as realistic as the Lilliputians, once we accept their world? Again, there are no easy answers to these questions, for we are dealing with an aspect of a basic assumption about the nature of literature, that concerning the viability of the mimetic theory of art, the belief that literature, and indeed all art, is rooted in the imitation of actual life. Although literature is not actually real life, it is clearly related to it —but how closely in actual practice is a moot question.

Still another problem, again one concerned with the actual practice of realism, is that of different "levels" of realism in a given work and the relations between them. Briefly, it is argued that a work can be highly unrealistic on the surface, yet very realistic indeed on a more profound level. For instance it could be argued that Shakespeare's historical inaccuracy about clocks in ancient Rome is unimportant in comparison to the psychological realism of the characterizations in *Julius Caesar*. But this argument can go much further than the mere excusing of error: profound levels of realism are attainable in literature, we are told, specifically because of a lack of realism on the surface, rather than despite it as suggested earlier. A surface lack of realism can be a means to an end, that of achieving various insights into human nature, for instance, or into some aspect of human experience which would not otherwise be easily accessible. If the transparent walls in *Death of a Salesman* and the various physical impossibilities in *Gulliver's Travels* enable us to see more clearly the nature of man, then they are fully justified according to this argument. Indeed, it has been further argued that the surface appearance of things is not the "true" reality, that it is merely a kind of illusion, like the optimistic front that Willy Loman, the salesman, presents to the world in order to hide his uncertainty. If a household can look normal, yet "really" be unusual, it will be difficult to perceive the more profound levels of realism simply by observing the external appearances. We must push these aside, we are told; we may ignore this level of reality or even distort it as Swift does if that will help us penetrate to the genuine reality that lies beneath.

Our last problems concerning realism are concerned with the reader's reception of realism or the lack of it, and these problems constitute important words of warning. The first, briefly, is this:

events and phenomena that are actually realistic may seem unrealistic to a reader if his experience does not happen to encompass them. Even well-educated readers sometimes feel that a particular character's actions are improbable because they themselves have never met anyone like him. Reading about such characters does not always help since we are all to some extent "from Missouri"—we have to see to believe, or to fully realize. For example, some readers have felt that the Duke in Browning's "My Last Duchess" could not have had the Duchess killed, because people don't really do such things—that is, these readers have had no experience with such people; for such readers the poem is entertaining, perhaps, but rather fantastic. But the fact is that people did do such things all too commonly in the particular time and place of the poem—during the Renaissance, in Ferrara, Italy. The remedy for this personal response to the poem is, first, to recognize that one's own experience is limited. Wider and more varied experiences will help solve the problem, but since they can never cover everything, a certain open-mindedness is always necessary.

The second word of warning is about the possible stock response due to our present general assumption that literature is normally realistic: since we are used to surface realism, we may be disconcerted, if not seriously disturbed, by a lack of realism. If this happens, we must be sure to ask whether the fault lies with the work or with ourselves: is the lack of realism the result of bad handling, or are we ourselves naively closing our minds to a valid literary technique? What are we to make of the ghost in *Hamlet* and the "elemental spirits" in Coleridge's "Rime of the Ancient Mariner"? The remedy lies in what Coleridge called "the willing suspension of disbelief for the moment." This does not mean that we should believe everything an author tells us, but that we should meet him halfway. Just what degree of realism is necessary depends on the particular work. We cannot always demand strict realism, for that degree is a convention that writers often ignore with good reason. We must accept or reject the degree and the nature of the realism in a given work on the basis of its own particular merits, for realism is a variable convention.

THE PROBLEMS ABOUT GENRES

The second major concept that concerns us in this discussion of literary convention is that of genres. Here we must deal with three crucial problems.

The first is an extension of a point made earlier about the nature of genres; it derives from the question whether genres are prescriptive or descriptive. Are the various genres we recognize a specification of the forms that literary works should properly fall into, or are they forms in which literary works at the present time simply happen to appear? Let us note briefly some of the ramifications of this question. In regard to the writer and particular works the question calls attention to the constraining effect of genre thinking. We wonder how often, and to what degree, particular works are written to fit specific genres and if such specification is due to a natural tendency for works to fall into categories, or to the writers' forcing their work into arbitrarily determined forms. We further ask if such possible forcing is beneficial or not: does it channel and thereby focus and intensify writers' efforts (as the sonnet form counteracted Wordsworth's tendency toward prolixity), or does it seriously cramp their styles? All art involves the selection and ordering of experience; from the writers' point of view, does it help to have that ordering directed from without, by the predetermined specifications of particular genres, or should each writer invent his own genres? The answer probably lies somewhere between the alternatives; the real problem is that of locating it within that area.

The second major problem leads us into the analysis of what specifications, what elements determine the particular genres. What characteristics of a given work define the genre to which it belongs? The answer, as René Wellek and Austin Warren indicated in *Theory of Literature,*[1] is twofold: the genre is determined by a work's "outer" form and by its "inner" form (its tone, its purpose, and so forth). Thus a sonnet is a fourteen-line poem in iamvic pentameter having certain rime schemes—this is its outer form; at the same time, it is a lyric poem, one which expresses the personal attitudes and ideas of an individual—this is its inner form. A genre can almost never be accurately defined in terms of one of its dimensions alone, as Wellek and Warren make clear: a sonnet used primarily for *narrative* is practically a contradiction in terms, no matter if it has the proper outer form or not.

One central practical problem, that of the relative importance of outer and inner forms, emerges when we consider, say, the genre of tragedy. For a long time it was maintained that tragedy was a form of drama—in other words, that its external form was dramatic, consisting of dialogue between characters to be presented on a stage. At present we do not consider this to be essential to tragedy. Instead, we depend for our generic classification on "inner" characteristics like the attitude toward experience, the conception of the nature of human life embodied in tragedy, permitting short stories, narrative poems, and novels to be included in the genre. The remaining "external" features that we conventionally expect in tragedy are more intrinsic than the dramatic form of presentation on a stage: the stature of the protagonist, the defeat or fall, the moral significance.

The same kind of problem arose on one famous occasion in connection with the poetic elegy. The problem was that of recognizing the essential features of the inner form. Conventionally, the elegy has always been defined externally as a poem having a measured rhythm, a moderate length, some variation in structure, and a serious tone; internally, it is clearly a lament over someone's death. But this conventional conception of its inner form though accurate as far as it goes, does not go far enough; the ultimate inner form

[1] New York, 1949.

of the literary elegy is the expression of philosophic attitudes or meditations on man and society expressed by means of the lament. Thus when Samuel Johnson, in the eighteenth century, attacked Milton's magnificent elegy "Lycidas" on the grounds that it was insincere, since the poet hardly knew the man whose death he was lamenting, the grounds for the attack were faulty because they were irrelevant: what is crucial in "Lycidas" is the views on art, religion, and mortality that it embodies, rather than the lament that occasions them.

Finally, to add a new perspective, we should note that other theories of genre classification have been advanced. Northrop Frye, for instance, argues that the ultimate basis for such classification is what he calls the "radical of presentation," that is, the theoretical relation between writer, work, and audience. Frye identifies four basic genres on this basis: drama, fiction, *epos,* and lyric. The first is seen on the stage by the audience, the second is read by the audience, the third is recited to the audience by the author, and the fourth is theoretically spoken by the author, alone. These root methods of presentation have various logical consequences and corollaries that encompass the various forms, both inner and outer, that we have been discussing. Perhaps these radicals of presentation will prove to be the "natural" bases for genres which critics have long wished to identify.

The last of our problems about genres is concerned with readers' attitudes toward the concept and toward the works it is applied to; it is thus analogous to the last problem about realism. The question is whether readers tend to think too narrowly in terms of the genres that are familiar to them. Despite the pleasure to be derived from the strange and novel, readers are often suspicious of unfamiliar or newly developed genres. These provide no means for them to orient themselves in relation to the material of the work (when we read a conventional plotted short story we know where we are, as it were), so that an unfamiliar genre seems artificial or may not be recognized as a genre at all. Many Westerners consider the Japanese *haiku* a contrived form of poetry (by definition it has three lines of five, seven, and five syllables successively), and many readers scorned Walt Whitman's free verse as formless when it first appeared. What such readers—indeed all readers—have to realize is that the most valid function of thinking in terms of genres is not to regulate the form and characteristics of literary works, but to enable us to relate the works to the traditions and conventions that constitute their literary context. When confronted with a work that seems to belong to no familiar genre we should not be tempted to throw it out, but should think of other works whose essential dimensions—the inner form as well as the outer—are similar, even if the works are different on the surface.

CLASSICISM AND ROMANTICISM—
THEIR POSITION IN CRITICISM

The classical and romantic polar attitudes toward human experience are dynamic, not static. Because they are general mental "sets," or basic principles, they are continually developing, being extended, or appearing in modified forms in differing situations. In their essences they remain constant, but under varying conditions they manifest themselves in various ways. It is our task now to explore some of the main ways they are manifested, and to recognize some correlative problems.

First, let us consider the problematic relationship between the classical-romantic polarity and the more specifically literary concepts that we have been considering. That relationship is ambiguous, and therefore gives rise to challenging speculations. Let us ask, for instance, if symbolism—compared to a more straightforward and explicit presentation of the theme—is typically a classical or a romantic technique, and envisage some of the resulting problems. Symbolism is romantic, some readers say, because the meaning remains elusive and ambiguous—the interpretation depends ultimately on the individual reader's response to the suggestive value of the symbols. Thus, in Blake's "The Tiger" the central image represents the wildness and ferocity of nature for some readers, while for others it symbolizes the power of evil, and for still others it stands for something else again. Those readers, on the other hand, who say that symbolism is classical point out that it manifests a process of generalizing experience, that it is a means of transcending particular things and events by making them represent more abstract phenomena. Blake's tiger is more than a single ordinary animal; when he asks, "Did he who made the Lamb make thee?" the poet shows that it is the kind of thing the tiger represents that he is concerned with.

Readers speculate similarly on the concept of genres. It is generally conceded that a writer or critic with a classical frame of mind tends to think in terms of established literary forms because of their definiteness, their orderliness—there was much respect for genres in the Neo-Classical period in England, for example. At the same time, an opportunity for speculation and indeed for research into literary theory develops when we consider the relationship between classicism and romanticism, on the one hand, and tragedy and comedy, for these genres embody another basic attitudinal polarity. Is tragedy romantic because of its intrinsic emotional element and its exalted conception of the significance of individual man, or is it classical (as evidenced by its importance in Greek literature) because it evinces a desire to face the truth, to confront even the worst in human experience rather than escape it? Conversely, is comedy basically classical because of its urbane and distant social perspective, or does its tendency toward escapism indicate that it is romantic? These are theoretical questions of profound importance; they are the kind of general problem that critics and students must recognize if they are to approach a comprehensive understanding of the nature of literature.

A second and more immediately functional relationship for us to consider is that between romanticism and classicism and actual literary works and writers. We ask, thus, about the immediate applicability of these concepts to particular novels, plays, and poems: does the romantic-classical polarity serve as a guide line in the interpretation and assessment of such works and writers?

It is legitimate, for one thing, for us to use this polarity descriptively, the way we apply generic concepts. That is, we say that a work is more or less romantic or classical depending on what relevant qualities it has. Wordsworth's "Tintern Abbey" we call romantic since it manifests a love of nature for its inspirational value, and because it insists on the importance of the individual's "mystical" interior experiences. But we cannot require a work to have all the characteristics of romanticism nor to avoid all classical tendencies completely. We employ these concepts to indicate relationships between similar kinds of works, not to classify them absolutely. Similarly, we identify the various writers in general terms as relatively romantic or relatively classical. Byron's marked individualism and his demonic and extravagant imagination lead us to consider him romantic. Yet in any assessment of him, we also have to take into account his powerful satiric verse, like the mock-epic *Don Juan,* his major work; this represents a strong classical tendency that prevents us from putting him and the other Romantic poets in one pigeonhole. Every writer, like every work, has connections with and differences from other works; the concepts of romanticism and classicism help us to understand those relationships.

Finally, those concepts help us to understand the different eras in literary history. The Neo-Classical and Romantic periods, as we know, are commonly described on the basis of tendencies in the literature and the general "climate" of opinion and attitude of the time. The same kinds of tendencies lead us to consider the Elizabethan period romantic: it manifested a faith in the importance of the individual as well as an interest in the strange and exotic. All Western literary history has been viewed from the perspective of the romantic-classical polarity; seventeenth-century France is considered classical, while the nineteenth century was romantic in both France and Germany, and the early nineteenth century was a romantic period in American literature. Despite the great variety of works and writers, and the atypical tendencies that we have to account for in these periods, we find romanticism and classicism to be very useful descriptive concepts.

The problem of identifying the character of a whole period is accentuated when that period is our own; we have a different perspective on the modern period—the late nineteenth and the twentieth centuries—than we have on earlier ones. What are the typical phenomena of our era, literary and otherwise? Are they evidence of a classical or a romantic climate of opinion? One romantic conception, that of the importance of the individual and of the worth of the common man, underlies much of modern life, specifically democracy and other political and social movements that are reflected in literature. At the same time, there is a classical motive behind modern science: the desire to establish general principles, to define patterns of phenomena that are universally reliable.

Let us concern ourselves specifically with literature, however. A particular feature fundamental to the literature of our period is the broad assumption of the mimetic theory of art, the idea that literature should represent real life accurately. Is the realism of our literature due to a classical desire to face human experience squarely, with common sense—to "see life steadily and see it whole"—or is it due to a romantic preoccupation with immediate and particular details, especially of common life, analogous to Wordsworth's devotion to the common man? The variety of possible answers is instructive in itself. As we become increasingly conscious of the complexity of the critical problems we deal with, our literary sophistication develops. Thus: realism may be romantic in one writer or work, and classical in another, depending on its function or the writer's intent; that is, it may be a vehicle for the subject matter (persons, places, events) which are treated more or less romantically or classically by different authors. Alternately, modern realism may combine both tendencies in a synthesis peculiar to our time. This is a problem that will exercise our powers of observation and analysis as our era advances.

To conclude our discussion, let us cite two more literary phenomena especially notable in our time—again, contrasting ones. These are the profound and persistent interest in literary theory and criticism on the one hand and the equally continuous experimentation by writers with different aspects of literary forms, functions, and techniques. The first interest represents an intellectual preoccupation with the general and the constant that betokens a classical frame of mind, while the second suggests the premium that romantics have always placed on novelty and originality. The critical faculty, highly developed in the literary field as we can see from the number of major critics and important critical developments in modern times, is at the opposite pole from the creative faculty, equally evident in such things as the continued development of kinds of prose fiction, the "theater of the absurd," and "beat" poetry. That such diversity in literary and philosophical tendencies exists in our era should please us greatly, for it is a sign of cultural vitality. Far from stagnating, our culture is active in many ways.

It is our job as critics and students to comprehend this cultural activity. To do so in the field of literature we must achieve a clear understanding of the elements of literature and the way they manifest themselves. And we must in the process maintain a balanced perspective on literary theory and the actual practice from which theory is derived. To assimilate and correlate validly the various works we read, we must continually further the interaction between literary principles and practices, guiding our studies of particular works by our knowledge of literary concepts, and testing the validity of those concepts in the light of particular works.

Appendix

APPROACHES TO LITERATURE

The following descriptions indicate the main ways students may be expected to study literary works, either singly or in combinations. Students can undertake some of these studies in ordinary preparation for class, and all are appropriate for papers and reports of many kinds. The approaches overlap in many ways, and all are important and critically valid, though particular students, like particular critics, will consider certain ones more valuable than others.

VERBAL EXPLICATION

A careful explication or examination of a work, or works, is a necessary preliminary to all other approaches. Its aim is to achieve a thorough understanding of the immediate content of the work. In the case of works written some time ago, we want to understand them as the author's contemporaries would have, as well as the way a modern reader does. To achieve this understanding is no small task; it demands close and careful reading. We have to follow the syntax and punctuation carefully, especially when reading poetry. We need to know the meanings of the concepts and images as the author uses them and of any allusions he makes; for this purpose, we have to read comprehensively and we often have to undertake research into historical contexts and intellectual or literary traditions. We must understand literary works well so that we will know accurately what we are talking about when we employ the other approaches; getting "the general idea" of a work is satisfactory only for the casual reader.

LITERAL INTERPRETATION

A literal interpretation treats literary works as direct embodiments or reproductions of life; we take the characters to be real people in real situations, and expect to "feel as if we were there" when reading about their adventures. The main interpretive techniques, then, are those we use in real life situations, in our own experience. The central focus is on the characters: we try to perceive what goes on in their minds, and to infer the varying interactions between the characters. For this task we need much psychological acumen, and also sharp perceptions of the details of setting and action as they bear on the characters. We can draw on our knowledge of ourselves, of other people, and of human nature in general, but we must beware of a personal response—many people and events in literature will fall outside our personal experience, so that we will have to suspend our disbelief. A literal interpretation is esthetically "naive," dealing with works "pre-literarily" as case histories, embodiments of humanly significant experience rather than as formed art. Yet we perceive many significant features in literary works through this approach: vividness of description, suspense and surprise in courses of action, strange or familiar kinds of people and events—all part of the works' being enjoyable as vicarious experience.

REFLECTIONAL INTERPRETATION

By this approach we treat literary works as reflections of concerns in some field commonly outside of literature, such as history, philosophy, and psychology. For the time being, the work becomes a specimen in that field. In literary survey courses, we often treat minor works as illustrations of one or another trend instead of reading them for their own sakes; in philosophy courses we even treat them as manifestations of ideas rather than works of art. Since literary works *are* important as social and historical documents, this approach is valid. The procedure for study is for us to start with, or acquire through research, a good grounding in the chosen field (philosophy, psychology, etc.), and considerable information about the particular concern (the concept of the Great Chain of Being, say) to which the work is relevant. Then, we examine the work (or works) from that perspective only. We need acute perceptions and powers of analysis for a rewarding interpretation, because the pertinent features of works appear in many ways: as themes (major or minor, overt or implicit), as arguments voiced by characters (directly or ironically), as implications of particular features of literary techniques, and in still other ways. Ultimately, we arrive at some perception of where the work stands in broadly human terms, though not specifically as literature or even as art.

ESTHETIC ANALYSIS

In an esthetic analysis we concern ourselves with literature as art; we assume, first, that each work as we have it is an artistic whole. Our aim is to define the work esthetically—to determine its precise nature as a work of art—and to determine how its nature is established by its structure, texture, tone, and other technical elements.

Two main courses of action are open to us. If we wish, we may begin with our general impression of the work's esthetic character and try to identify the features most responsible for that character, continually examining the various literary elements for consistency or variant effects. Alternately, we start with a systematic consideration of the literary elements in the work, aiming at correlating them to arrive at a conception of the total nature of the work; this method is especially effective when we are faced with difficult or puzzling works. Both methods aim at a total æsthetic conception of a work. Occasionally, we will want to perform a partial analysis as a means of gaining insight into some aspect of literary art; we will then examine particular works as noteworthy manifestations of that aspect ("My Last Duchess" for characterization, for example). In order to articulate this central critical approach to literary art, we must understand thoroughly the various elements of literature to begin with, and must then ask ourselves what is the precise function of each as it appears in the particular work.

REPRESENTATIVE INTERPRETATION

Always, we want to know what a work "means," whether that meaning is like the specific moral of a fable or a generalized and vague attitude toward life. The interpretation of literary works operates on two levels of representation.

The first level is that of thematic interpretation. We assume that works have central themes, explicit or implicit, for they all represent human experience directly or indirectly. If we start by approaching a work literally (as described above), we will find that the embodied experience is not unique, that other experiences are likely to follow the same pattern or to have the same effect: this fact points toward a thematic significance whether or not this is identified clearly by the author. The study technique we use, therefore, is to generalize from the particular instance: we ask ourselves what *kinds* of characters are involved, and what the over-all nature of the action is. In the process we take into account the significance of any symbols presented to us, especially since some works depend primarily on symbolism. We will need some background knowledge to understand these symbols, especially if they are private ones of the author's.

The second level of representation is that of archetypal or mythic interpretation. This representation emerges from a secondary level of symbolism in contrast to the immediate level dealt with in thematic interpretation. We push the generalizations further, and in a different direction, looking for types of characters and patterns of action common to the literature of a given culture. Our purpose is to understand literary works in terms of their connections with the rest of the literature of their culture. When we encounter a tragic work in which the main character is excluded from society, we try to determine how it is connected with other kinds of tragedies and how it differs from them: this leads us to a perception of a kind of "cultural" meaning in particular literary works and ultimately for literature as a whole. Mythic interpretation involves our acquiring and bringing to a work a good deal of knowledge of other literature and particularly of archetypes and mythic patterns of action. Then, we must be very careful and perspicacious in relating to them the characters and events of the given work. If we undertake this in general terms, we often find that interpretation is easy, but not very meaningful; a detailed and significant analysis demands much of us.

EVALUATION

It is practically impossible for us to avoid forming some opinion about the worth of literary works. But we want to know how such an opinion can become a judgment. Evaluation comes logically after the other approaches have prepared us for it: we must understand a work thoroughly and accurately before we can legitimately

judge how good it is. And we must also have a clear understanding
of our standards of evaluation; the commonest general standards
operate roughly as follows. We judge the worth of a work as literary
art by deciding if the various literary elements and techniques are
effective; we judge the moral worth by deciding if good is promoted
and evil opposed; and we judge the "truth" of a work by deciding if
it advances an understanding of man and his realm. We must always
be careful to read a work in a valid way, and wholly and profoundly,
and must apply those standards that are relevant to the given work
(we do not condemn "My Last Duchess" for its lack of lyric beauty,
for instance).

An evaluation may in the last analysis be an expression of our
tastes, but it will be a validly reasoned expression if we base it on a
profound comprehension of the work and of the standards we apply.

INDEX

233